Discover how to control y
and unlock 30 hours of lost time a month

SMART

TIME MANAGEMENT
FOR DOCTORS

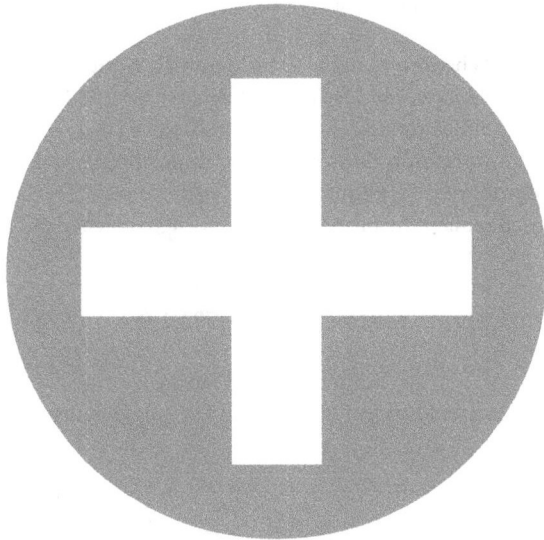

KATE CHRISTIE

SMART Time Management for Doctors

Proudly self-published in Australia by Kate Christie in 2017

First edition

kate@timestylers.com
www.timestylers.com

ISBN: 978-0-9925792-1-0

Editor: Robert Watson
Cover and Internal Design: Pipeline Design (pipelinedesign.com.au)

Disclaimer: The material in this publication is of the nature of general comment only, and does not represent professional advice. To the maximum extent permitted by law, the author and publisher specifically disclaim any liability, loss or risk which is incurred as a consequence, directly or indirectly, of the use and application of any contents of this work.

Contents

Thank you!

Thank you to everyone who provided support, guidance and motivation while I was writing *SMART Time Management for Doctors*. This includes the medical practitioners who completed the Medical Time Management Survey, sharing their insights on how they manage their time, as well as those who read my drafts.

Thanks also to Dr Mukesh Haikerwal, former President of the Australian Medical Association for his opening comments.

To my editor, the uncompromising Robert Watson who kept me on my game with unrelenting consistency and humour. And to my wonderful mentor and coach, Andrew Griffiths, for your inspiration.

Very, very special thanks to Dr Brian Hsu who embraced my vision to help time-poor doctors everywhere gain greater control over their time and encouraged me to write this book. Your support, friendship and sponsorship have been invaluable.

Finally, to Freddie, Wally and Peggy who every day give me the love and encouragement to continue to live my dream of being an Author, Speaker and Coach.

Kate x

Foreword

He that has time has life — English Proverb

When I finished reading this practical, clearly written, witty and "oh so true that it was painful" instruction book on how take back your life, I smiled at an irony! My newfound manual – which suggests saying *No* – saw me saying *Yes* to writing this Foreword. I did because Kate's book provides excellent guidance to doctors on how to reclaim time which can then be spent with their families.

As a passionate and vocal advocate for my profession, my colleagues and our patients for over 30 years, the health, mental health and well-being of doctors has been a core theme. Our patients, our families and indeed we depend on these being in good shape so that we can be effective and successful in our sacred Hippocratic traditional caring. I continue to advocate on these themes and have written extensively about challenges in medicine today.

The volume of current health knowledge and information, speed of medical developments and constant technological evolution are impossible to remember and must be handled and processed in new ways. The demands and expectations upon us to be available to deliver for our patients and the constantly evolving face of modern medicine all contribute to the frenetic pace at which doctors work and live.

As medical practitioners, our ability to effectively manage our time is a critical skill. Time management is central to success as a junior doctor, vital in establishing and maintaining a practice, necessary to continue to study and embrace medical developments, core to interaction and collaboration with peers, imperative to undertake continuous professional development, and indispensable as we continue to meet the expectations of our patients.

Doctors have always worked long hours, under immense pressure in demanding and competitive environments. There is now evidence for and recognition that "burnout", emotional and physical exhaustion and mental illness are major impediments to a happy and successful life.

I have juggled many roles including President of the National and State Australian Medical Association, the World Medical Association Chair of Council, Chair (and current Board member) of the Beyond Blue Doctors' Mental Health Taskforce, with an active practice and family life. I am well aware of the need to address mental health issues and physical wellness in the profession through paying greater attention to factors such as better workplace conditions and embedding work-life balance.

I am absolutely thrilled that Kate Christie has written a book which shines the light on the unique time management challenges faced by doctors. Her 5 SMART Steps is a logical and simple to follow framework which all doctors can use to regain significant over their time. I commend the skill, tenacity and veracity of this book which is pithy, punchy and can fulfil its intention of helping us doctors reclaim some of that precious time!

Mukesh Haikerwal,
Former President of the Australian Medical Association

Introduction

Be not afraid of growing slowly. Be afraid only of standing still — Chinese Proverb

You work in a profession where, despite the best efforts to plan your working week, your daily activities are dictated by circumstance rather than strategy. You have learnt to be reactive rather than proactive. In addition, your industry is highly regulated which means you need to allocate regular time to more mundane, yet mandatory, activities to ensure you maintain the appropriate level of compliance.

How do you find the time for everything you need to do? How do you find the time for a life outside work? How do you do it all?

Doctors are time poor, sick of the constant juggle, and live with an ever-present undercurrent of stress. Something needs to change so that you can be a great doctor and live a more integrated work/life. However, the irony is that you are simply too time poor to devote the time needed to make a significant change to your current time management habits.

Since you have bought this book on time management for doctors, you are clearly acknowledging the need to manage your time differently.

Several years back I developed a framework to help busy professionals and business owners better manage their time: *The 5 SMART Steps*. Thousands of people have been educated on how to apply *The 5 SMART Steps* to their circumstances.

But doctors are unique. I can't even count the number of hours I have spent in Emergency Waiting Rooms, doctors' rooms, and Fracture Clinics with my three children who over the years have had more than their fair share of broken bones and accidents and, in one particularly alarming period, were literally glued and stitched together. I genuinely sympathise with the pressure, the workload and the unique time demands on doctors that I have witnessed. This prompted me to write *SMART Time Management for Doctors* to provide specific time management advice to benefit you, your family, your business and your patients.

More so, I had already had the pleasure of working with Brian Hsu, an Adult and Paediatric Spine Surgeon based in Sydney, Australia, to coach him through *The 5 SMART Steps*. While working with Brian I was quickly struck by the particular and often extraordinary time management challenges doctors face. The medical field, more than most, is reactive and driven by the needs of others, which makes it very difficult to plan and organise time. *The 5 SMART Steps* made a considerable difference to how Brian now manages his time, his medical practice and his other business interests. It has allowed him to identify the activities he can delegate, reject or do differently, buying him back hours of lost time and ensuring he is now able to use all of his time well. The framework also allowed him to find the time he needed to ensure he could spend time with his family and on his own wellbeing.

You can achieve these results too. SMART Time Management is a learned skill. This book won't waste your time on the warm and fuzzy or on theoretical explanations for why poor time management occurs. Rather, you will be given practical, logical and easy-to-implement time management strategies which, when repeated consistently, will become the habits which take your success to the next level.

So, jump in. It's time to start managing your time differently.

How to use this book

Nobody is born wise — African Proverb

Unlike regular self-help business books which present information for you to think about, *SMART Time Management for Doctors* is a workbook which involves more than just thinking. You need to invest time in order to find your lost time.

In Part A you will apply *The 5 SMART Steps* to your own unique circumstances. There are a number of exercises to complete which begin by digging into your underlying challenges and drivers, then build to what habits to change and how to change them. The key to your success is being totally frank and honest, especially in the early exercises, and then letting go of poor habits and replacing them with much better new habits in the later exercises. Letting go is the hard part for many people, but that's where the big gains will be made. The exercises can be completed:

- ⊙ in this, your copy of *SMART Time Management for Doctors*

- ⊙ in your *Doctors Workbook*, a free copy of which you can download at www.timestylers.com. The *Doctors Workbook* exactly mirrors the exercises in this book and includes a worked-up example of how the fictional Dr Alex works through *The 5 SMART Steps* and completes the exercises.

On completion of Part A you will reclaim hours of lost time.

As a bonus, Part B includes a number of the strategies and tools I use with my clients to take the control of their time to an even higher level.

The frameworks, concepts and strategies covered in *SMART Time Management for Doctors* can be used by other professionals in the medical or allied health industries.

PART A

....

Let's talk SMART

Starting is half the task — Korean Proverb

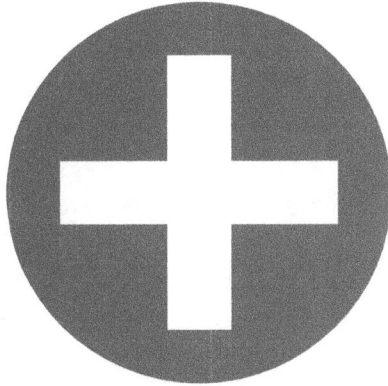

The Framework: what is SMART?

The best time to plant a tree was 20 years ago.
The second best time is right now — Chinese Proverb

Many of the Time Management Challenges doctors face are common to most professions:

Examples

- *interruptions*
- *procrastination*
- *setting the right priorities*
- *poor planning*
- *failing to delegate*
- *not setting or maintaining boundaries*
- *lacking focus*
- *not saying No*
- *lacking time for administration and paperwork*

The list goes on.

And some of your Time Management Challenges are unique to your profession:

Examples

- *being on-call*
- *life-threatening and emergency scenarios*
- *extensive periods of time juggling study with paid work*
- *managing multiple teams or clinics*
- *the need for Continuing Professional Development*
- *the need to stay current with new medical knowledge and technological advances*
- *the often unpredictable length of clinical tasks*

This list goes on too.

The 5 SMART Steps will work you through a series of exercises to ensure you gather the right data on your personal time management habits. You will be asked to apply your own critical analysis to this data, with a view to reframing your time and the way you manage your Practice. And you will establish your own frameworks to help entrench these new time management habits.

The end result? You will gain control of your time and find and harness hours of lost time.

Sounds easy, right? Well, *yes* and *no*. Without question you could design, test and then implement your own time management framework. However, you don't have the time to do this. Moreover, while there is genuine value in a well thought out framework, the implementation step is often the kicker. As a doctor, you know this better than anyone. You can clearly and convincingly explain to your patients the lifestyle and habitual changes they need to make to live a better and healthier life, however you can't actually make them do it. Implementation is up to the patient. This book provides productivity strategies to make implementation as simple as possible, guiding you towards a successful outcome.

There is rigour in *The 5 SMART Steps* and you will find yourself challenged as you examine – and then reshape – your habits and the way you manage your time at work. I also encourage you to implement *The 5 SMART Steps* across the rest of your life: at home, in the community, your volunteer work and spiritually. In short, this is a contemporary process to help you track, rate and cost your time, and then set up a series of simple and sustainable strategies to ensure you manage your time the SMART way.

So, let's talk SMART.

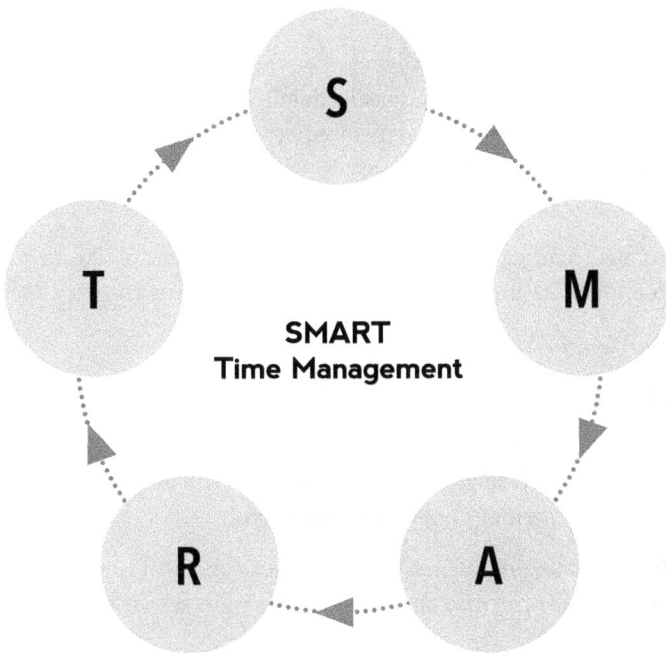

S

M

A

R

T

SMART
Time Management

S = SELF-AWARE

The first step to managing your time smarter and getting back quality time is to become self-aware. In Step 1 you will identify your:

⊙ Key Time Management Challenges: what keeps tripping you up?

⊙ Core Values: what values drive your behaviour?

Why? Because you need a baseline against which to reflect on your current time management habits, and to benchmark against the improved behaviours you implement.

M = MAP

In Step 2 you will Map three days in detail. Think of it as a personal time management audit. You will clearly identify where you currently spend your time and you will give some thought to what just one *better* day would look like.

Why? Because you can't know what changes you can make to your time management habits unless you know in detail where you currently spend your time.

A = ANALYSE

In Step 3 you will Analyse your Mapped time across Four Task Categories: your Musts, Wants, Delegates and Rejects. You will also identify what your current time management habits are costing you.

Why? Because categorising and costing your time will give you the clarity you need to better prioritise and focus on the right activities.

R = REFRAME

In Step 4 the data you have collected in the first three steps comes together. You will identify exactly the tasks you can do smarter, faster, or not at all.

Why? Because identifying everything you can personally Delegate or Reject, as well as business processes and daily practices which can be improved, will allow you to find hours of lost time.

T = TAKE ACTION

The last step is implementation. You will schedule deadlines for implementing actions, ensuring you embed and sustain your new time management behaviours to your daily routine. This is where the rubber hits the road.

Why? To ensure your success!

- -

The act of finding and then harnessing your lost time will take commitment, discipline and personal accountability.

So, commit now. You have nothing to lose except your poor time habits. What you will gain back is hours of time to do what you love: more time to reconnect with family and friends, more time to spend on your own health and wellbeing, and more time to strategically build the next stage of your success.

Busy – it's a disease

By the time the fool has learned the game,
the players have dispersed — Ghanaian Proverb

Before jumping into Step 1 of *The 5 SMART Steps,* a quick word about everyone's favourite buzzword:

BUSY!

When you run into a colleague and they ask how you are, you tell them you are *busy*. They respond that they are *busy* too! And then you both discuss the general *busyness* of every other doctor you know.

Busy, it appears, has acquired significant social status.

But don't be fooled. Being Busy, or Busyness per se, is not a badge of honour. It's an insidious, time-sucking disease, and it's time to call busyness for what it is: a *boiling frog*.

Essentially, or so the story goes, if you put a frog into a pot of boiling water it will instantly jump out because it detects immediate danger. However if you place the frog in cold water and slowly raise the temperature the frog won't perceive the danger and it will slowly cook.

The boiling frog is a useful metaphor for our inability to react to threats which slowly sneak up on us. In this case, an overwhelming sense of busyness. It's not like you can pinpoint in your diary the day that busyness suddenly happened to you, is it?

And yet, like the frog, you are slowly cooking.

You are taking on more and more, rushing from one thing to the next, and your work and life have become a juggling act. Dash to work, write up a report, see your patients, check your emails, more patients, paperwork, more patients, surgery, rounds, more paperwork, return phone calls, face-to-face consults, over-the-phone consults, hallway consults, check emails, make calls from the car, dash home to see the kids before bed, study, wave to your partner as you fall into bed … and get up and do it all again.

You have so many balls in the air that it's only a matter of time before you start dropping a few. And as a doctor, are there really any balls you can afford to drop? Probably not. As a result, you work longer hours to ensure you fit it all in. That in turn means significant compromises in other areas of your life: family, friends, exercise, personal interests and sleep all come off second best.

This busy lifestyle is taking its toll. Doctors, more than most busy professionals, at least understand the health risks – both mental and physical – associated with functioning at this pace and under this level of pressure for a prolonged period of time.

The good news is that busyness is a lifestyle choice. You have a choice: to continue to live this way or to take control of your time.

The water is boiling and it's time to jump out of the pot.

Step 1

SELF-AWARE

Before you score, you must first have
a goal — Greek Proverb

The first step to maximising your productivity is Self-Aware, where you will reflect on your current habits and behaviours. The closer you examine your personal Point A (where you are right now), the faster and with greater chances of sustained success, you will reach Point B (the place you want to be, a place of significant and serious time management control).

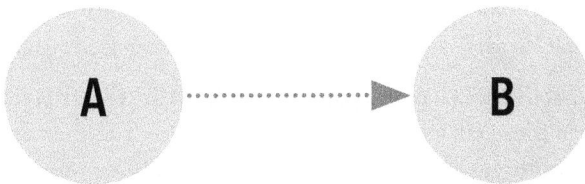

A ·········▶ B

You already have a degree of self-awareness about your time management habits. You know you have competing priorities and responsibilities, most of which seem to have an equal level of urgency. You are trying your best to get everything done and (mostly) you do it all (fairly) well. While some tasks have been almost permanently parked in the *Too Hard Basket*, nothing (too) significant has fallen through the cracks. You may not be in full crisis mode (yet), but at the very least you acknowledge that there is room for improvement.

From a triage perspective you are unlikely to be rushed straight through for emergency treatment, but you certainly need some first aid.

At the end of Step 1: Self-Aware you will have absolute clarity around:

⊙ Your Key Time Management Challenges; and

⊙ Your Core Values.

Identifying your Key Time Management Challenges

He that neglects time, time will neglect

— Spanish Proverb

The three most common Time Management Challenges doctors face are *Unpredictable Hours, Competing Priorities* and *Long Hours of Work*. These three challenges may resonate with you, or you may have other challenges. Moreover your Time Management Challenges will change over time depending on your level of seniority, where you are at in your career, whether you are still studying, the role you are currently in, whether you have a partner and/or children, the age of your children, and so on.

So, what keeps you awake at night? When you wake at 3.03am what do you dwell on? What do you worry might have fallen through the cracks?

The act of self-reflection is not something we often do. Mostly, and ironically, this is because there isn't enough time. Perhaps it's also because there is a degree of discomfort as to what a little self-reflection might reveal. Regardless, as you have committed to changing your time management habits, now is the perfect time to visit the *Room of Mirrors* and take a good hard look.

Complete Exercises 1.1–1.4 below to identify the time management challenges you most need to focus on. It may well be that the above three challenges resonate strongly with you, but even so, undertake the exercises below to ensure real clarity.

EXERCISE 1.1

Diagnostic –
My Key Time Management
Challenges

Examine the statements below and tick each one you can relate to as a Time Management Challenge. This is not an exhaustive list so include additional challenges which are of significance to you.

Time Management Challenge	Yes, that's me
It annoys me that I don't have enough time	☐
I have too many competing priorities which frustrates me	☐
My hours are unpredictable which makes it hard to plan my day	☐
I am constantly interrupted which makes for a longer day	☐
I can't find the time to grow my practice and this plays on my mind	☐
I manage multiple teams and it's a constant juggle	☐
I don't spend enough time with my family which makes me feel guilty	☐
Being on-call adds a layer of complexity and results in fatigue	☐
I don't get enough sleep and feel constantly tired	☐
I struggle to say No which means I take on too much	☐
It's hard to find the time to research and write papers	☐
I work all of the time, and enough is enough!	☐

I juggle work with study which leaves little time for other pursuits	☐
I am constantly jumping from one task to the next and back again	☐
I am not well organised and this frustrates me/my team	☐
I don't spend enough time with my partner which worries me	☐
I am too busy to stop, and if I do, everything piles up	☐
I am overwhelmed by governance requirements	☐
Diary management is not a strong point for me	☐
I am a bit of a procrastinator, so it takes me a while to get started	☐
I don't have time for myself and I always put myself last	☐
I have way too much on my plate	☐
My To Do List has its own heartbeat	☐
I struggle to stay on top of key medical developments which troubles me	☐
I don't have time to review and update my business processes, so I don't even know how inefficient I am	☐
I lie awake at night worrying about what might have fallen through the cracks	☐
Parental responsibilities mean I don't have the time I need to focus on my career	☐
I ...	☐
I ...	☐

My Key Time Management Challenges

Of the statements ticked or written above, the three things I find *most* challenging when it comes to managing my time are:

1. _____

2. _____

3. _____

How do I feel right now?

After reflecting on your answers in Exercises 1.1 and 1.2, how do you feel about this life you are living? Are you stressed, guilty, tired, happy, calm, annoyed, frustrated, overwhelmed, worried, resigned, motivated? Are your work relationships strong? Are your non-work relationships strong? Are you healthy?

How do you feel?

I feel ...

_____

_____

_____

_____

Example

Dr Phillip approached Step 1: Self-Aware with a level of trepidation. At 45, his tendency was to just get on with things without giving too much thought to the habits which were driving his behaviour. However, he knew he had time management habits which annoyed his team (... and his wife) because they told him so! So, he jumped in.

Three years down the track, Dr Phillip revisits Step 1 on an annual basis. He says it keeps him honest about the time management issues which currently challenge him (as these change over time or old habits sometimes creep back) and to ensure he knows exactly what he needs to focus on to maximise his productivity.

EXERCISE 1.4

What one thing would I change?

If you could fix just one of the challenges identified in Exercise 1.2, which one would you choose, and why? This is important. There is no point in drafting a long laundry list of all the things you need – and want – to change. Why? Because the longer the list, the more likely it will be to join the other mundane, onerous tasks currently sitting in your *Too Hard Basket*. To set yourself up for success, choose just one thing to be your immediate point of focus:

My one focus: _____

Why? _____

_____

_____

The point of self-reflecting in the first of *The 5 SMART Steps* is so you know where you are right now. Moreover, once you reclaim control of your lost time, you will have the satisfaction of looking back at your responses above to see how far you have come.

Bottom line: if you don't tweak your time management habits now, then, in the very least, getting to the next level of success in your career, having a healthy life outside work, and achieving everything you want to achieve will be a longer, harder climb. The ultimate risk is that you might not get there at all.

My Wants List – what will I do with my extra time?

On completing *The 5 SMART Steps* you will have found and reclaimed a lot of lost time. The whole point of SMART Time Management is to have the skills and discipline to identify the right tasks to do at the right time and to complete these efficiently, freeing you up to spend more time on the things you love. With that in mind, start a list of what you will do with that reclaimed time. Cast your mind wide; this doesn't have to be all about work.

Example

I want to jog three mornings a week

I want to learn Italian

I want to travel more

I want to attend school sports days to watch my kids

I want to spend more time practising my guitar

I want to coach my daughter's basketball team

I want to mind the grandchildren every Friday

I want a weekly date night with my partner

I want to volunteer at the local care facility

I want to undertake more study

My Wants List: What will I do with my extra time?

_____

_____

_____

_____

_____

_____

_____

_____

_____

_____

_____

Print out your draft Wants List and place it somewhere visible. Being able to do all the things on your Wants List is the reward for reframing the way you use your time. Your Wants List will be revisited in Step 4: Reframe.

With your draft Wants List front of mind, it's timely to think of what really motivates you day in and day out.

Identifying your Core Values

Every task you perform, every action you take, and each decision you make is guided by an internal set of personal Values. Complete exercises 1.6-1.9 to identify the Values you stand for: the principles, beliefs and moral compass which guide your decisions, including how you choose to spend your time.

What is most important to me?

Consider your day-to-day behaviours. These are the things an observer would see you focussing on over the course of many weeks. Complete the sentences in the *Your Response* Column in the Table below providing as many examples as you can. Do not complete the *Value* Column at this point; that comes shortly.

There is an example in the Table in italics below, illustrating how to complete this exercise. As a reminder, download the free *Doctors Workbook* from www.timestylers.com. This will allow you to look over the shoulder of Dr Alex to see how she completed these exercises.

Sentence	Your Response	Value
I am happiest when ...	*I am faced with an emergency scenario which I resolve with a best case outcome for the patient and their family.*	
I am happiest when ...		
I get a deep feeling of pride when ...		
I would spend a free hour on ...		
I feel most energised when I am ...		
In my favourite room I surround myself with ...		
When I daydream, I dream about ...		

If I was to receive a compliment I would want it to be about …	
When I initiate a conversation, I like to talk about …	
The things I won't compromise on are …	
I worry most about …	

Let's connect the dots.

Understanding your Values and identifying what is most important to you is key to helping you plan your time, establish your daily priorities, focus your efforts on what is significant, say No to the low priority activities and stop chasing the distractions.

What is most important to you will help you plan your time. Reflecting on and then articulating your Values will help you gain clarity on the people, the work and the lifestyle outcomes you most want to spend your time on.

So, what are your Values? It's time to think about exactly what drives your behaviour. Below is a list of common values, many of which may resonate with you.

Common Values:

Adventurous	Career-oriented	Competitive
Ambitious	Caring	Consistent
Assertive	Charitable	Contented
Balanced	Committed	Cooperative
Brave	Community-minded	Courageous
Calm	Compassionate	Creative

Curious	Healthy	Resourceful
Dependable	Helpful	Respectable
Determined	Honest	Responsible
Diligent	Independent	Self-controlled
Discreet	Innovative	Selfless
Efficient	[Of] integrity	Self-reliant
Empathetic	Intelligent	Sensitive
Enthusiastic	Just	Spiritual
Entrepreneurial	Kind	Spontaneous
Ethical	Knowledgeable	Strategic
Expert	Loving	Strong
Fair	Loyal	Successful
Faithful	Original	Supportive
Family-oriented	Patient	Talented
Financially-secure	Positive	Team-oriented
Focussed	Powerful	Thoughtful
Frugal	Practical	Trustworthy
Fun	Private	Understanding
Generous	Professional	Valiant
Good	Prudent	Visionary
Happy	Reliable	Virtuous
Hard-working	Resilient	Wise

EXERCISE 1.7

My Values

Defining your Values sounds simple enough and many people can automatically reel these off when asked. However, your Values aren't generally what you *say* they are. Rather, they are revealed by how you *behave*.

You aren't driven by just 2 or 3 Values. You are likely to have many Values which come into play each time you make a decision or take an action. While most of these will remain constant throughout your life, there will be some which change in their level of importance depending on your stage of life and what is happening around you.

Review each of *Your Responses* in Exercise 1.6 and then, in the *Value* Column, assign the Value from the *Common Values List* which best describes each of *Your Responses*.

From a time management perspective, you need to get this right because having absolute clarity over what drives you is central to deciding exactly where you should – and shouldn't – spend your time.

> **TIP**
>
> The words you choose for your Values aren't restricted to those on the *Common Values Table*. Those are just examples to get you started. You can adjust those words or use different Values that you already know you have.

EXERCISE 1.8

My List of Values

Read over the Values you have identified in Exercise 1.7 and list them below. Group together those which are obviously similar.

My List of Values:

- ❯ _____
- ❯ _____
- ❯ _____
- ❯ _____
- ❯ _____
- ❯ _____
- ❯ _____
- ❯ _____
- ❯ _____
- ❯ _____
- ❯ _____
- ❯ _____
- ❯ _____
- ❯ _____
- ❯ _____
- ❯ _____
- ❯ _____

TIP

Dr Alex struggled a little doing this exercise. See how she worked through this in the *Doctors Workbook*.

Exercises 1.6 and 1.7 have allowed you to convert your day-to-day behaviours into a long list of Values. However, right now, you need to home in on what is absolutely non-negotiable for you – your Core Values.

This will take some serious reflection, so don't skate over this. Examine your Values with honesty and rigour. You don't have to share your answers with anyone, however if you are feeling courageous, ask those who know you best what they think your behaviour says about you and your Core Values. Their responses might possibly be alarming but will certainly be eye-opening.

My Core Values

Based on your List of Values in Exercise 1.8 distil the list down to your 6 to 8 non-negotiable Values. This can be hard. You may have identified 20 Values all of which on first glance resonate strongly with you. If so, you can undertake the exercise in two parts: boil it down to 12 to 15 Values now, and then revisit your list in a few days, after you have had time to mull it over, and then have another cull to get your list down to 8 or less.

> **TIP**
>
> Consider which of your Values are so alike that you can blend them together. For example:
>
> Trustworthy, Ethical, Honest, [Of] Integrity: could be captured as just *Ethical*
>
> Innovative, Entrepreneurial, Visionary: could be captured in the single value *Innovative*

My Core Values:

- ❯ _____
- ❯ _____
- ❯ _____
- ❯ _____
- ❯ _____

❯ _____

❯ _____

❯ _____

Example

After serious reflection, Dr Jackson identified seven Core Values, of which three were Family-oriented, Professional and Successful. These came from his responses to the following statement: I get a deep feeling of pride when I am ...

- *being a great father and husband (Core Value = Family-oriented)*

- *being well regarded by my colleagues (Core Value = Professional)*

- *being highly successful in my field (Core Value = Successful)*

However, his behaviour showed that he was working +70hrs a week and only had time with his kids on Sundays.

On its face, while his behaviour fulfilled two of his Core Values, there appeared to be a serious misalignment between what Dr Jackson wished to be a Core Value around family time versus how he actually behaved.

This exercise was not about judging Dr Jackson. It was about helping him recognise that while all three Values are solid Core Values to hold, being successful (at work) and well regarded (at work) had a higher level of focus for him at that point in time.

Dr Jackson hadn't previously considered this. Initially he was alarmed and embarrassed. Was he a bad dad, he asked? No! His Core Values were absolutely fine. He didn't need to change them. What he needed to do was to continue to follow The 5 SMART Steps to allow him to learn how to work smarter, ensuring he retained his fantastic success and reputation at work, while also freeing up time to spend with his family.

This exercise helped Dr Jackson hit the pause button, re-adjust and to start living a life that included everything which was most important to him.

Nice work! You have identified the Core Values which are most critical to you. These are the Values which drive your behaviour and against which you can set your future priorities and make decisions as to where you will spend your time.

Write these up or print them out and pin them on the wall next to your Wants List so that you can consciously make decisions about where you spend your time, at work and play, which are consistent with your Core Values.

If, like Dr Jackson, reflecting on your Core Values leaves you with terrible guilt that, for example, your family time is not where you want it to be, that does not mean that *Family-oriented* needs to be deleted from your list of Core Values. It just means that now you know that your current behaviour does not truly reflect your Core Values. Don't be alarmed! This is not a bad revelation. It will help inform where you do and don't want to spend your time in Steps 3 and 4.

When your Core Values come into conflict - work or life?

You have a lot of things you desire out of your work life, your private life, your family life and your spiritual and community lives. From time to time these desires will come into conflict with one another. When this occurs you need to make a choice and your Core Values will help you make this choice. This will often involve identifying what is most important at any given time and focussing on that first.

Example

Dr Eleanor identified eight Core Values, of which three were Compassionate, Financially-secure and Family-oriented.

In order to display Compassionate, Dr Eleanor initially increased each appointment time by 10 minutes to ensure her patients did not feel rushed. However, after one month of this new practice it became clear that if she was to continue in this vein she would either have to accept fewer patients onto her books [and compromise her Core Value of Financially-secure] or she could retain the same number of patients and work longer hours [compromising her Core Value of being Family-oriented].

After checking the data, Eleanor found that only 20% of her appointments could be classified as a longer consult, while 50% of appointments ran to time and 30% ran under time. She decided she did not actually need to continue with her adjustment to appointment times to be true to her Value of being Compassionate as this mix of longer/shorter/on time appointments was one she could work with.

However, she did decide to close her Practice at 2pm each Friday and every second Wednesday to allow her to spend time with her kids (Family-oriented) without materially impacting her Value of being Financially-secure.

What would you do in the same situation?

The concept of Work/Life Balance is a myth. Your task is not to perfectly balance all aspects of your life by giving equal weight to all of your Core Values at any one time; that simply can't be done. Rather, your task is to use your Core Values as the compass to guide how you juggle your competing priorities, ensuring you effectively integrate all of the important areas of your life.

You work and you love it. You have a life and you love that too. You love to do lots of things. Often your work crosses over into home or you take your work 'on the go' while you watch the kids at sport, or you handle minor 'home' issues while at work. No-one spends exactly equal amounts of time, joy or endeavour on their work life as they do on their non-work life. Work is simply a part of life and life is a concoction of all of the various tasks performed each day. We all strive to comfortably integrate all of these needs.

Instead of chasing the illusion of Work/Life Balance, embrace Work/Life Integration and give yourself permission to spend your time where it is most needed (by you or others) at any given time. That might be on the tools, with your family, pursuing personal development, or simply spending time on the other many elements of your life.

Checklist: Now You Know

- [ ] Your Key Time Management Challenges.
- [ ] How you feel about your time spend.
- [ ] Your Core Values: the drivers which help guide the decisions you make and where you choose to spend your time.
- [ ] Your need to ensure that all aspects of your life are integrated.

Keep your Core Values list at hand as you will refer to this again in the next Steps.

It's time to Map your time.

Step 2

MAP

*You'll never plough a field by turning it
over in your mind — Irish Proverb*

By now you will have decided to reject *busyness*.

This is a good decision, given that another symptom of a busy lifestyle is
the inability to clearly articulate what it is you do each day that makes you
so busy. This isn't an unusual phenomenon. However, how can you expect
to move away from your busyness and start managing your time smarter,
including rejecting all of your time-wasting habits, if you don't know in detail
exactly where you spend your time?

To ensure you get the data you need, Step 2: Map will have you undertake
a personal time management audit. Over a 3-day period, including one day
of the weekend, you will Map your time in 10-minute intervals to ensure
you capture every phone call, email, interruption, coffee break and so on.
Without exception, those who Map their time with this level of detail
consistently achieve much more impactful results than those who adopt a
less rigorous approach. And while those who are more studious often report
how irritating the Mapping process can be, they are amazed at how life-
changing their results are. So, suck it up and just do it.

At the end of Step 2: Map, you will have a clear idea of:

⊙ What a Typical Day looks like for you; and

⊙ What a Better Day would look like.

Why Map?

Every single day seems to be as full and demanding as the one before. It never, ever stops. You never, ever stop. You are constantly accessible via portable devices that you don't switch off until you fall into bed each night ... and not even then if you are on-call.

But do you actually know what you do all day as you busily buzz about like a blue-arsed fly?

Monitoring and measuring where you currently spend your time is key to improving how you manage your time. Why? Because until you know exactly how you spend your time, how can you possibly know what you need to change? This involves:

- ⊙ Recording every task you perform over a given period and how long each task takes;

- ⊙ Recording the time and duration of each interruption, distraction and occasion you jump from one task to another; and

- ⊙ Taking note of when you feel most energised during the day and the times when you feel flat or you lose concentration.

The Time Sheet below is an extract of the template you need to use to Map your time. You can print as many Time Sheets as you like in the *Doctors Workbook* at www.timestylers.com.

	1	2	3	4	5
Time	Task	Dur Mins	Must/Want/ Delegate/Reject	Financial Cost	Other Costs
5am					

	1	2	3	4	5
6am					
7am					

3 Typical Days

For 3 days (including one weekend day) take note (in Column 1 Task) of everything you do from getting up, making breakfast, showering and getting dressed, kids stuff, travelling time, time spent on social media, emails, client consults, liaising with colleagues, researching, studying, having lunch, every interruption, every phone call, every pager alert, and everything you do at home from the dishes, washing the clothes, supermarket trips, making meals, eating meals, cleaning, tidying, socialising and so on. You get the picture. It's all about the detail. Be honest. If you spend an hour on Facebook on the commute to work then record it. Now is not the time to fudge the data.

Record the amount of time you spend (in Column 2 Duration Minutes) on each task. Do not estimate your time or write down the time you *wish* you had spent on the task. That is ultimately unhelpful.

Take your Time Sheets with you when you are on the go and fill them out in real-time. It is a mistake to get to the end of the day and try to recreate your day. You will forget the filler tasks you undertook, the interruptions you received, and you will generally under-estimate how long you spent on tasks.

At this stage you only need to complete Columns 1 and 2 of the Time Sheets (the other Columns will be completed in subsequent Steps and as such are shaded below). An example of completed Columns 1 and 2 is set out here in italics:

Example

	1	2	3	4	5
Time	Task	Dur Mins	Must/Want/ Delegate/Reject	Financial Cost	Other Costs
5am	*Waking up*	*5*			
	Shower and clean the shower tiles	*10*			

		1	2	3	4	5
	Check emails	15				
	Breakfast	15				
	Get dressed	15				
6am	Drive to work listening to radio	40				
	Park car, walk to office	10				
	Grab coffee, log on	10				
7am	Emails	15				
	Chat to Jim re shift change	5				
	Emails again	10				
	Call from Jane re kids drop off/pick up	10				
	Review paper for conference	20				

This Exercise will take you 3 days, however the more data you have the better, so feel free to Map additional days.

Dr Alex in the *Doctors Workbook* has completed a set of worked Time Sheets available for you to view at www.timestylers.com. You can follow her thought process as she has also annotated her Time Sheets.

Example

You will recall in the example in Step 1: Self-Aware, Dr Eleanor identified the Core Values of Compassionate, Financially-secure and Family-oriented. In order to display being Compassionate, Dr Eleanor initially intended to provide longer consult times for all patients. However, after examining the data she found she did not need to take this step.

The data she relied on came from her Time Sheets. After she Mapped 3 days across a Typical Week, including exactly how long each and every consult took, she was able to make an informed decision that enough of her consults ran to or under time to compensate for the 20% which ran overtime.

Start filling in the Time Sheets tomorrow morning and return to this book on Day 4.

TIP

Your Time Sheets will provide a wealth of data. For example, be aware of the times of day when you feel most energetic and the times you feel tired. Monitor your energy levels over the week and you will see a clear pattern. This will come into play later.

Day 4: Are you serious?

It's Day 4 . You can stop Mapping your time. You have the data you need.

Looking over your Time Sheets can be a little alarming. The first thing you might think is: *Wow I do a lot!* or *Look at how productive I am!* Some of you might even think: *I am spending a lot of my time on a whole lot of crap!*

> **TIP**
>
> Don't confuse a jam-packed week with a productive week.

Regardless of first impressions, the important thing at this stage of *The 5 SMART Steps* is not to judge yourself. The whole point of working through each exercise is to gain control over your time by identifying your poor time management habits and then implementing proven strategies to reclaim your lost time. Don't give up.

Neither should you be too quick to pat yourself on the back. Busyness does not mean you are productive and it certainly doesn't equate to being efficient. But more on that later. For now, trust the process.

EXERCISE 2.2

My Energy Flow

Consider your Time Sheets, and with your knowledge of your personal energy flow each day (*are you a morning person? a night owl?*) note below your high energy times of the day and your low energy times. You will come back to this data point later.

Energy Levels	Times of the day
I have High Energy	
I have Low energy	

Design a Better Day

You now have a feel for how a series of typical days in a typical week look for you. For a change of pace in Exercise 2.3 you will design a *Better Day*. Imagine how different things could be. How would a Better Day pan out for you? This is not dreamland where you own Sunshine Island and sip cocktails from dawn to dusk. This is a Better Typical *Working* Day.

Below is a Better Day time sheet where you only include what would make your day better: from a half-hour sleep-in, a morning jog, a day where each patient turns up and all consults run on time, no emergency scenarios, home in time to say goodbye to the cleaner who has left the house spotless, the washing done and the family meal cooked, your partner is happy, the kids aren't fighting, and you all sit down to eat together. It still requires work tasks and home tasks, nicely integrated for your current situation.

Your Core Values are key here. Make sure you reflect back on these (they are pinned on the wall next to your Wants List, right?) and only incorporate into your Better Day tasks which reflect your Values.

Time	My Better Day
5am	
6am	
7am	
8am	
9am	
10am	

11am	
12noon	
1pm	
2pm	
3pm	
4pm	
5pm	
6pm	
7pm	
8pm	
9pm	
10pm	

Take a few minutes to compare a Typical Day from your Time Sheets with your Better Day.

While you can see that your Better Day looks pretty damn fabulous, it is also a little hard at this point in time to see how you are going to get from Point A to Point B. Don't worry! Continue to follow the framework. You are right on track.

Checklist: Now You Know

- [ ] Exactly where you spend your time each day over 3 Mapped days.
- [ ] The times of day when you have High or Low energy.
- [ ] What a Better Day looks like. This is what you are working towards.

Keep your Time Sheets handy. It's time to Analyse the wealth of data in your Time Sheets.

Step 3

ANALYSE

You don't have time to do everything.

When it comes to managing your time the SMART way, and finding and harnessing hours of lost time, it is not enough to just conduct a time audit of your week (Step 2: Map). You also need to slice and dice the data and genuinely question where you spend your time and what can be discarded or done differently.

Having completed 3 days of Time Sheets, you now need to have a good hard look at them to consider:

⊙ Where are you actually spending your time?

⊙ What could you let go of?

⊙ What could you do differently?

⊙ What are your current time management habits costing you?

At the end of Step 3: Analyse, you will:

⊙ Have dissected the tasks you typically perform (as identified from Step 2: Map);

⊙ Understand what your current time management habits are costing you; and

⊙ Have calculated how many lost hours you can reclaim.

> **TIP**
>
> Step 3: Analyse is broken into two parts. If you are on a roll and reading Step 3 in a High Energy period then go for it and work straight through in one sitting. If, however you want to reflect as you go, tackle Step 3a first then complete Step 3b after a break of a day or two.

Step 3a: Task Categories – categorise your time

Hour by hour time departs.
— Italian Proverb

Every single task you perform can be assigned to one of Four Task Categories: your Musts, Wants, Delegates and Rejects. These are set out in the table below with examples under each Category in italics:

The Four Task Categories

MUSTS	WANTS	DELEGATES	REJECTS
The activities you have to do.	The activities you love to do and would love to do more of.	The activities you currently do but which could be done by someone else.	The activities you don't need to do at all (or which you could do differently).
Shower	*Rock climb*	*Paperwork/administration*	*Attending meetings you*
Eat	*Fish*	*Office/process review*	*don't need to attend*
Teach	*Bike ride*	*Some patient consults*	*Checking your email alerts*
Consult	*Music festivals*	*Admin-related emails*	*every time you hear a 'ping'*
Team meetings	*Read with the kids,*	*Attending some meetings*	*Keeping social media open*
Commute	*attend assemblies,*	*Draft paper preparation*	*while you are working*
Board meetings	*go to sports days*	*Bookkeeping*	*Washing clothes*
CPD	*Meditate & Pilates*	*Scheduling patients*	*that aren't dirty*
Parent-teacher	*Dinner parties &*	*Draft blog*	*5 trips to the*
interviews	*Date nights*	*Basic procedures*	*supermarket a week*
Teacher meeting	*Cook*	*Team management*	*Browsing through*
Accountant meeting	*Attend an International*	*Clean*	*your junk mail*
Present at conferences	*Conference every 2nd year*	*Iron*	*Doing anything*
	Write a book exploring	*Garden*	*during peak hour*
	medical advancements	*Shop*	*Face-to-face banking*
	in my field	*Food preparation*	*Fridge gazing (instead*
	Start a blog	*Clean up after the kids*	*of meal planning)*
		Take out the bins	*Allowing interruptions*
		Walk the dog	*Too Hard Basket*
			Piling (instead of filing)
			Killing time
			Saying Yes all of the time

There are four exercises below designed to help you:

⊙ identify the tasks you Must do, those you Want to do, and those you could possibly Delegate or Reject; and

⊙ stay motivated in your quest to reclaim hours of lost time.

My Task Categories

Work down Column 3 of your Time Sheets and quickly label each task which is clearly a Must, Want, Delegate or Reject. Leave any task which requires more thought and then address that task after you have dealt with the no-brainers.

In some cases you might feel that a task falls into more than one category. Where there is an overlap, consider which category intuitively has the stronger pull for you and allocate the task to that category. Equally, there may be some tasks you feel obliged to allocate to a Must or Want by virtue of pure guilt. This is a trap. Be honest. If you don't enjoy a task then that's a pretty good indication that it is up for grabs as a Delegate or Reject.

When it comes to tasks you could possibly Delegate, think of tasks which can be done by:

⊙ Someone you don't have to pay, such as a partner, child or grandparent. For example: your partner can help with household chores; kids from the age of 3 are definitely capable of clearing the dinner table; kids who are 6 and older are happily capable of a whole lot more; and

⊙ Someone you do need to pay. For example: invoicing, paperwork, tax documentation, housekeeping, cooking, ironing and so forth.

When it comes to Rejects, think of the tasks:

⊙ You can stop doing altogether because they are a waste of time; and

⊙ Which need to be done but which could be managed more efficiently with some tweaking.

Just because you identify a task as something that you might be able to Delegate or Reject does not mean you have to actually delegate or reject it. Record it as a possibility for now, as the actual process of Delegation and Rejection will be undertaken later. Moreover, this is an iterative process; you will continue to come back to your Time Sheets in the next Steps as you become clearer on your Musts, Wants, Delegates and Rejects.

The running example extract is below, with Column 3 now completed.

Example

	1	2	3	4	5
Time	Task	Dur Mins	Must/Want/ Delegate/Reject	Spend $	Cost Layer
5am	Waking up	5	M		
	Shower and clean the shower tiles	10	M		
	Check emails	15	W		
	Breakfast	15	M		
	Get dressed	15	M		
6am	Drive to work listening to radio	40	M		
	Park car, walk to office	10	M		
	Grab coffee, log on	10	W		
7am	Emails	15	M		

	1	2	3	4	5
Chat to Jim re shift change		5	M		
Emails again		10	R		
Call from Jane re kids drop off/pick up		10	R		
Review paper for conference		20	M		

Off you go to do yours now. Remember to refer to Dr Alex's example for further guidance.

Example

Dr Christopher takes a coffee break and stands in the kitchen while the kettle boils. Dr Samuel is also in the kitchen. They exchange pleasantries and then Dr Samuel takes the opportunity to run a patient scenario past his colleague. Later Dr Christopher allocates this time to a Want (he wanted a coffee break). Dr Samuel decides to allocate this time to a Must as he gained some useful feedback from his colleague.

Example

Dr Ahn's daughter wants to be a ballerina. Dr Ahn takes her to lessons and stays to watch. This takes up 2 hours of her week. Dr Ahn admits to herself that she would really rather poke her eye out with a stick than watch 35 five year olds frolic in tutus, and that she has been staying at the lessons out of guilt. The other parents seem to love it! Dr Ahn bites the bullet and allocates this time as a Reject. Her plan is to walk her daughter into lessons, stay for 5 minutes to make sure she is settled and then adjourn to the cafe next door where she will use the remaining time to either catch up on work (a Must) or catch up with a friend (a Want).

My Summary Tasks and Time Spend

After completing Column 3 of your Time Sheets, it's time to consolidate. Pull the data from Column 3 of your Time Sheets into the Table below noting each task under its relevant Task Category.

As you consolidate, add up the total amount of time you have spent on each of the Four Task Categories across the 3 days - your first time cut - which will give you a picture of how many hours you could reclaim if you Delegate and Reject every task you have earmarked as up for grabs.

Print out your completed Summary Tasks and Time Spend Table and post it next to your computer for easy reference. This will be much easier than constantly referring back to 3 days worth of Time Sheets. An example of the time cut is in italics.

Task Category	Tasks	My First Time Cut (with the time mapped in 3 days extrapolated over to 7 days)
Musts	*patient consults, team meetings*	*85 hours 45 minutes*
Wants	*jog, time with kids*	*15 hours 10 minutes*
Delegates	*cleaning*	*5 hours 50 minutes*
Rejects	*Social Media*	*4 hours 5 minutes*

Great work! You now have a summary of the tasks you perform and you know how much of your time you spend on your Musts, Wants, Delegates and Rejects. Typically, you can expect to see that the vast majority of your time is being spent on your Musts, with a lot less time being spent on your Wants. The question is: How do you move to a place where you can spend more and more time on your Wants?

Easy.

By focussing on what you can Delegate and what you can Reject.

EXERCISE 3.3

How many hours could I reclaim each year?

Following your First Time Cut in Exercise 3.2, it's interesting to look at the time you could reclaim each year if you ultimately Delegate and Reject every task you have identified as a Delegate or a Reject. Nothing is set in concrete as yet, but do the maths because it's a great motivator. An example is in italics below (with 3 days worth of data extrapolated over to 7 days and then a year):

		Example	Your answers
A	Delegates: The number of hours I would save each week if I Delegated everything I have identified as a possible Delegate	*5hr 50m* *(5.8hr)*	
B	Rejects: The number of hours I would save each week if I Rejected everything I have identified as a possible Reject	*4hr 5min* *(4.1hr)*	

Calculation:

(A + B) x 52 weeks = the number of hours I could reclaim each year	$(5.8 + 4.1) \times 52 =$
	515 hours per year

- *if you work 40 hrs/ week you just regained 13 weeks a year!*

- *if you work 50 hrs/ week you just regained 10 weeks a year!*

- *if you work 60 hrs/ week you just regained 8 weeks a year!*

If Step 3a doesn't motivate you to take action to smash this out of the park, then Step 3b – where you calculate what your current time management habits are costing you – could well horrify you. More so, how can you find time for your own health and wellbeing, to spend with family and friends, or to just 'be'?

For those of you who need a break, pause here and come back to Step 3b tomorrow.

Step 3b: What are your time management habits costing you?

> Wasting time is robbing oneself
> — Estonian Proverb

At a minimum you have studied for four years to work in your area of expertise. Many of you have also taken on additional years of specialty training. All of you are regularly undertaking Continuing Professional Development. You have worked hard to grow your success. But time is short. You know from your Time Sheets that your schedule is full. There is no room for more. And it doesn't matter how talented you are, if you don't have any time left to give, how can you take your success to the next level? Your current time management habits represent a big risk to your ongoing success. How so? Because regardless of how well you are managing your time, your habits (and your tolerance of the habits of those around you) are costing you.

> **TIP**
>
> If you are already pretty good at this stuff, then at the very least, you can raise your time management proficiency even higher.

An effective use of your time is where the vast majority of your time is spent on your Musts and Wants. Most likely, however, what you have discovered in completing Step 3a is that the way you currently use your time is not always the best use of your time.

And just what is this costing you? Probably a whole lot more than you thought.

The Four Cost Layers

As always, you want good data, not guess work. To make this work, you need to understand exactly what your time is worth so you can:

- ⊙ maintain your motivation to implement new time management habits and strategies;
- ⊙ start valuing your time accurately; and
- ⊙ decide whether any given activity is really the best use of your time.

There are Four Cost Layers to consider in calculating the costs associated with how you manage your time:

Cost Layer	Definition
Financial Cost	The cost to you in dollar terms of each activity you perform.

Lost Opportunity Cost	Each time you decide to do something, you are deciding *not* to do something else; there will always be a trade-off. The Lost Opportunity Cost is the option(s) you gave up when making your choice.
Emotional Cost	Where you strongly feel the activity you chose to undertake is a good/poor use of your time.
Physical Cost	Where the activity you chose to undertake takes an associated mental or physical toll.

Think of the Four Cost Layers as layers of a cake. Just as each time you cut the cake and you see the four different layers, each time you choose to undertake a particular task, there will be four potential costs you incur.

Generally, one of the Four Cost Layers will resonate with you more deeply than the others. If so, this is the Cost Layer you should focus on as you continue to Analyse your Time Sheets (and the tasks you choose to undertake going forward).

Cost Layer Number 1: Financial Cost

> An ounce of gold will not buy an inch of time
> — Chinese Proverb

Your time is money. As such your Financial Cost is the cost to you in dollar terms of each task you perform.

Before you complete the next two Exercises, the scene is set in the following example.

Example

Dr Kayne is a GP who earns $97.60 per hour. For the sake of this exercise, Dr Kayne rounded up his hourly rate to $100.

After Analysing his Time Sheets, Dr Kayne calculated what his tasks across a Typical Week were costing him financially on an annual basis. Some of these costs are extracted below. In particular, Dr Kayne was alarmed to see what his social media habit was costing him, let alone the cost of undertaking administrative tasks himself.

Task	Duration (over 7 Days)	Annual Financial Cost @ Dr K's hourly rate of $100
Social Media/ Internet Surfing	*7hr*	*7 hours x $100 x 52 weeks = $36,400*
Administrative tasks (only on work days)	*15hr*	*15 hours x $100 x 52 weeks = $78,000*
Cleaning the house (each Sunday)	*4hr*	*4 hours x $100 x 52 Sundays = $20,800*
Lost time (30min each day)	*3.5hr*	*3.5 hours x $100 x 52 weeks = $18,200*
		Total Financial Cost per annum $153,400

The total above represents the annual Financial Cost of just four tasks Dr Kayne was spending his time on. Feeling motivated to calculate your costs now?

The dollar value of my time

Contact your Accountant and ask them to calculate your personal hourly rate based on last year's tax return. Like Dr Kayne, round the figure to make your calculations simple.

My hourly rate is $............

Costing the tasks I perform

Quickly work your way down Column 4 of your Time Sheets and calculate the financial cost of each task you have performed over the 3 days you Mapped (the running example is shown in Exercise 3.7).

Next, return to your First Time Cut in Exercise 3.2 (extracted below). Using your hourly rate, complete the Financial Costs column to calculate your total financial cost for each of the Four Task Categories over 7 days, and then complete the Annual Financial Costs column to calculate your financial cost over the course of a year.

Example

	Example	Financial Cost	Annual Financial Costs	Your time spend (extra-polated over to 7 days)	Your Financial Cost	Annual Financial Costs
Musts	85hr 45min	85.7 x $100 = $8570	$8570 x 52 = $445,640			
Wants	15hr 10min	15.2 x $100 = $1520	$1520 x 52 = $79,040			
Delegates	5hr 50min	5.8 x $100 = $580	$580 x 52 = $30,160			
Rejects	4hr 5min	4.1 x $100 = $410	$410 x 52 = $21,320			
		Total =	$576,160		Total =	

Confronting? Good!

> **TIP**
>
> Many of the tasks you identified as Musts and Wants could be Delegated (that is, Outsourced) to someone else who is an expert in their field, for a lower hourly rate than yours. Wouldn't it make sense to reconsider whether such tasks would be better earmarked as a Delegate, or at least identify them as being up for grabs? Hold that thought, as you will come back to this in Step 4: Reframe.

Assuming you repeat most tasks day in and day out, you may well have been spending many hours (and many dollars) performing tasks that no-one would dream of paying you for at your hourly rate.

If the Financial Cost layer is a hot spot/motivating factor for you, then this is the question you need to constantly ask yourself: *Is this the best use of my time?*

Cost Layer Number 2: Lost Opportunity Cost

Time is the one loan that no-one can repay
— Chinese Proverb

Unfortunately, your Financial Cost is not the worst of it. As you keep cutting through the cake, the next layer of cost you incur is your Lost Opportunity Cost.

While we all have the same 24 hours a day, how you allocate, manage and then use your time in each of those hours will be very different.

Lost Opportunity Cost is associated with anything of value (financial or otherwise, such as a lost benefit or a lost pleasure) that you give up to acquire or achieve something else. Put simply: your trade-offs.

Extending Dr Kayne's example, in addition to the Financial Costs he was incurring, he needed to consider the Lost Opportunity Costs associated with how he was spending his time.

Example

Dr Kayne's Tasks and Time Spend	Dr Kayne's Financial Costs	Dr Kayne's Lost Opportunity Costs
1 hour per day on Social Media/Internet Surfing	*$36,400*	*1 hour he could have spent: at the gym, meditating, with his family, research/Continuing Professional Development*

3 hours per work day on administrative tasks	*$78,000*	*3 hours he could have spent on myriad strategic, partnership, networking opportunities or taking on additional patients*
4 hours cleaning the house each Sunday	*$20,800*	*4 hours of time for himself, a long lunch with friends, catching up with family, playing sport*
An accumulated 30 minutes of unused pockets of time each day	*$18,200*	*Time to tackle the Too Hard Basket*

If the Lost Opportunity Cost layer resonates most strongly with you, then when it comes to choosing where to spend your time, keep asking yourself this: *What is the trade-off? What else could I be doing which I will gain greater benefit from?* If the trade-off isn't worth it and the Lost Opportunity Cost is too great, make a better choice.

Cost Layer Number 3: Emotional Cost

Time wastes our bodies and our wits; but we waste time, so we are quits — Anonymous Proverb

The Emotional Cost of how you choose to spend your time is a huge issue for those who try to juggle career success or business growth with lifestyle responsibilities. Emotional Costs invariably play out where the tasks you choose to spend your time on are in direct conflict with specific Core Values. Most often, there is a constant tension between your drive to succeed vocationally and your desire to be a great parent, friend, partner, community member or whatever the case may be. Emotional Cost is whether you feel you spent your time well or not. These costs generally include feelings of stress, guilt and worry about whether you made the right choice.

You can see how this plays out for Dr Alex in the *Doctors Workbook*, particularly how she feels about her Core Values.

By way of example, this is what Dr Kayne considered:

Example

Dr Kayne was cleaning his house out of habit but it caused him enormous frustration. Plus he spent half the time yelling at his kids to help, which left him angry and his kids resentful. His emotional costs included frustration, anger, annoyance, and later guilt at having yelled at his kids. His kids then played on this guilt, making him feel manipulated!

TIP
If you spend 14 hours a day working and your children are in bed asleep by the time you get home each day, there is likely to be an Emotional Cost associated with this, for both you and the children. This is time you will never get back.

Cost Layer Number 4: Physical Cost

Death will cure all pain — Sicilian Proverb

The final cost layer is Physical Cost. This one isn't rocket science. With Physical Cost, you need to listen to your body. If you are spending time on tasks which cause you physical discomfort, or outright pain, or which impact your mental health, then the tasks are exacting a Physical Cost (on top of your other costs) that may no longer make sense to you.

Example

Dr Kayne was shocked when he gave focussed consideration to what his time management habits were costing him physically. His list included stress-related headaches, making poor dietary choices, too much alcohol and too little exercise, all of which had resulted in weight gain. In worrying about this, he was also losing sleep.

EXERCISE 3.6

Bring my costs together

Costing out your time using the Four Cost Layers allows you to stress test whether any given task is the best use of your time. For every single choice you make about how you spend your time, there will always be a Financial Cost and a Lost Opportunity Cost. Other decisions will involve three or even all Four Cost Layers.

The Cost Layer that is most impactful will differ for each individual who reads this book. Your aim is to decide which Cost Layer resonates most strongly with you, then use that Cost Layer to test whether you are choosing the best tasks to spend your time on and whether those tasks align to your Core Values.

And remember, not all time is created equal. Some tasks, such as choosing to watch your kids play sport or to go on a date with your partner instead of spending an additional two hours at work, may not be the best use of your time financially, however you will gain enormous happiness and satisfaction from your decision (again, think Core Values). Other tasks, such as sitting at your desk without a break might result in a clean patient slate for the day, but is not necessarily the best use of your time physically/mentally (again, think Core Values).

Your Financial Costs are already listed as Column 4. Review Column 1 of your Time Sheets and reflect on whether any of the tasks you perform are exacting another cost you are no longer prepared to accept. Complete Column 5 using the following legend for simplicity:

OC: Lost Opportunity Cost

EC: Emotional Cost

PC: Physical Cost

For any task you initially identified as a Must or a Want, but which you now feel is costing you too much (either in a Financial, Lost Opportunity, Emotional and/or Physical sense), consider whether you can change these tasks to a Delegate or a Reject. Mark up any changes to Column 3.

At this point, don't worry about how you are going to achieve the switch from doing the task to not doing the task; that will come shortly. For now, you simply need to have a clear view of what you want to stop doing because the cost(s) no longer makes sense. Continuing with the running example:

Example

Time	1 Task	2 Dur Mins	3 Must/Want/ Delegate/Reject	4 Financial Cost	5 Other Costs
5am	Waking up	5	M	$8.50	
	(Shower and clean the shower tiles) ~~M~~ D → *Delegate the tile cleaning*	10	~~M~~ D	$16.50	PC
	Check emails	15	~~W~~ R	$25	OC
	Breakfast	15	M	$25	
	Get dressed	15	M	$25	
	radio/use time for CPD ↖ *(Drive to work listening to radio)*	40	~~M~~ R	$67	OC
6am	*current route but pick up coffee on the way* →				
	(Park car, walk to office)	10	~~M~~ R	$16.50	OC
	Grab coffee, log on	10	W	$16.50	
7am	*(Emails)* → ~~M~~ R *Don't start my day on emails!*	15		$25	OC
	Chat to Jim re shift change	5	M	$8.50	OC
	Emails again	10	R	$16.50	OC
	Call from Jane re kids drop off/pick up	10	R	$16.50	
	Review paper for conference	20	~~M~~ D	$33	OC

Having reflected on your Musts, Wants, Delegates and Rejects in light of your Costs (and quite possibly having made some changes across the Four Task Categories), the next step is to test your updated Musts, Wants, Delegates and Rejects against your Core Values.

A quick stress test of my tasks against my Core Values

Refer to the Core Values you identified in Step 1: Self-Aware, a copy of which you have displayed on your wall. Living and working in a way which is consistent with those Core Values is key to your happiness. Why? Because if your daily behaviours and tasks are inconsistent with your Core Values, there is a conflict, and this will impact your happiness, along with your levels of guilt and anxiety.

If the majority of your time spend does not reflect your Core Values you need to adjust where you spend your time.

Keeping your Core Values in mind, cast your eye down Column 3 of your Time Sheets and against each task you have identified as a Must or a Want, consider whether you are being true to your Core Values. Circle any task which is inconsistent with your Core Values.

Next, make sure you have not earmarked for Delegation or Rejection a task which is strongly aligned to your Core Values. If you have, the task is actually a Must or a Want and you need to realign it. Circle these anomalies as appropriate.

On completion of Exercise 3.7, you may decide to move some of your Musts to Rejects or move some of your Musts to Delegates or vice versa. That's OK; this is what a quick stress test is all about.

Continuing with the running example:

Example → *Family time: adjust to leave after I see the kids'*

	1	2	3	4	5
Time	Task	Dur Mins	Must/Want/ Delegate/Reject	Financial Cost	Other Costs
5am	Waking up	5	M	$8.50	
	Shower and clean the shower tiles	10	MD *Delegate the tile cleaning*	$16.50	PC
	Check emails	15	WR	$25	OC
	Breakfast	15	M	$25	
	Get dressed	15	M	$25	
6am	Drive to work listening to radio	40	MR	$67	OC
	Park car, walk to office	10	MR	$16.50	OC
	Grab coffee, log on	10	W	$16.50	
7am	Emails	15	MR *Don't start my day on emails!*	$25	OC
	Chat to Jim re shift change	5	M	$8.50	OC
	Emails again	10	R	$16.50	OC
	Call from Jane re kids drop off/pick up	10	R	$16.50	
	Review paper for conference	20	MD	$33	OC

radio/use time for CPD

current route but pick up coffee on the way

Analysing where you spend your time, and what your choices are costing you, can be challenging. You are breaking down your time and analysing it to within an inch of its life. It's bound to be confronting. You are almost there and this is the good part.

My Second Time Cut – are you serious?

With all Columns of your Time Sheets now complete, revised and stress tested, calculate the number of hours you have identified as lost hours you can reclaim.

Write your Second Time Cut here, carrying across from your First Time Cut in Exercises 3.2 and 3.3.

	My First Time Cut (transfer your answers from Exercise 3.2)	My Second Time Cut (extrapolated over to 7 days)
Musts		
Wants		
Delegates		
Rejects		

The above data accurately represents where you spend your time and, importantly, how many hours you can reclaim if you Delegate and Reject every task you have identified as being tasks which you now know are not the best use of your time.

Let's make this even better.

How many hours will I reclaim over a year?

Take the data from your Second Time Cut and calculate below how many hours you will reclaim over the course of a year:

	Total Time Reclaimed
The number of hours I would save each day if I Delegated everything I have identified as a possible Delegate	
The number of hours I would save each day if I Rejected everything I have identified as a possible Reject	
Total Hours Reclaimed	

WOW!

Step 3: Analyse has taken a lot of considered work. You have added significantly to your personal data set around your time management habits. You have also created an enormous amount of momentum and motivation to ensure you convert the data collected into reality.

You are well placed for the final two Steps of *The 5 SMART Steps*. You are about to reclaim hours of lost time.

Excited?

How do I feel?

Write down a few thoughts about how you feel right now:

I feel:

_____

_____

_____

_____

_____

_____

_____

_____

Checklist: Now You Know

☐   Your Musts, Wants, Delegates and Rejects

☐   Your Financial, Lost Opportunity, Emotional and Physical Costs

☐   You have undertaken a quick stress test of your Musts, Wants, Delegates and Rejects against your Core Values

☐   You have calculated how many hours you can reclaim by Delegating and Rejecting selected tasks

Take a break.

When you return to Step 4: Reframe, have your printed Table from Exercise 3.2 at hand. You are almost there.

Step 4

REFRAME

Time longa dan rope — Jamaican Proverb

At first glance, the potential number of hours you identified in your Second Time Cut (Step 3: Analyse) may seem to you to be a little, well, extraordinary. This is understandable because it's all academic at this point. However, don't forget that those potential time savings reflect what is up for grabs should you choose to delegate and reject every single task you have identified as a Delegate or Reject. You may not choose to make every single change. And yet, even if you find and harness just one hour of lost time a day, imagine the difference that will make. That's a whole working week each year!

You have already gained real clarity over your Core Values, your Four Task Categories (Musts, Wants, Delegates and Rejects), and the Costs (Financial, Lost Opportunity, Emotional and Physical) associated with your current time management habits.

In Step 4: Reframe, you will:

⊙ identify exactly what you are going to Delegate at work and at home;

⊙ identify exactly what you are going to Reject at work and at home; and

⊙ build on your list of Wants.

We are creatures of habit, waking and falling into the flow of the day, each day, in much the same way as the day before and the one before that. As such, the key is to understand which of your habits impact your ability to manage your time well. These habits must be discarded in favour of better habits which allow you to focus on the right tasks at the right time in order to produce sustained excellent results.

Establishing a new habit and genuinely locking it in takes six weeks of repeating that habit every day. That can be a hard slog, but the reward is that the new habit then becomes second nature to you. If you do the work, you will gain control over your time.

Reframe – SMART Delegation at Work

> A fool is thirsty in the midst of water
> — Ethiopian Proverb

The reason you Delegate the things you don't want to do, don't have the skill set to do well or efficiently, or don't have time to do, is to give yourself time for the things you do want to do. Go figure.

At work, for those of you with an established support team, the key is to Delegate effectively, including providing clear instructions on the task, the outcomes required and the delivery date. How to Delegate the SMART way is outlined in detail later.

TIP

For those of you without an established support team, think outside the box:

- Are there more junior doctors you can involve in projects or tasks to increase their knowledge/experience?
- If you work at a hospital is there a central administration or support team you can draw on?
- Is it time to employ (permanent full-time or part-time) or engage (casually or on a contract basis) an Administrative Assistant?
- Are there tasks you could outsource to a Virtual Assistant (either based onshore or offshore)?
- Can you train appropriate allied health staff to undertake some aspects of your work for you?

It's time to determine exactly what you intend to Delegate.

SMART Delegation at Work

You may already Delegate some activities at work. However you can see from your Time Sheets and the Delegates quadrant in your Summary Task and Time Spend Table (Exercise 3.2) that there are additional tasks you can pass on to someone else to free up your time for more important or enjoyable tasks.

If you have an established support team, you can add to your Summary Task and Time Spend Table by asking your team to identify any tasks you currently perform which they believe they could effectively (with or without additional training) undertake for you. These would be tasks which you didn't encounter during your 3-day audit.

At this stage of the process don't worry about how you will actually delegate the tasks; this will be covered shortly.

Using your Summary Task and Time Spend Table from Exercise 3.2 complete the Delegation List below (or in your copy of the Doctors Workbook), by identifying every task you know you would derive a benefit by Delegating it at work. It might be because you don't enjoy the task, it takes too much time, or someone else can perform it faster, better and more economically than you. For each task you identify, select the date (deadline) by which you will have Delegated the task and to whom. Keep a running record of the time you will reclaim. Refer to the Doctors Workbook for Dr Alex's worked-up example for guidance (an extract is in italics below).

Delegates at Work	Date	Who	Time Reclaimed
Daily/Weekly Activities			
Taking phone calls			
Making phone calls			
Sorting my Inbox			
Making appointments			

Delegates at Work	Date	Who	Time Reclaimed
Monthly/Annual Activities			
Invoicing			
Tax			
Irregular Activities			
Research			
Drafting papers			

Remember Dr Kayne from Step 3: Analyse? This is what he considered:

Example

Dr Kayne decided to address his habit of completing his administrative tasks himself. Initially he had chosen to undertake the paperwork because he felt that his knowledge of his practice and patients meant he was saving time (and money) in doing the work himself. Over time however, completing the paperwork had become a habit; he continued to do this low value work simply because that was what he had always done. He now knew better.

His administrative tasks were taking him 3 hours a day and included filing, sorting through emails, maintaining his patient schedule, preparing documentation for his accountant and paying his tax.

Dr Kayne didn't enjoy any of these tasks, however he had a choice:

A. *He could continue to undertake all of the administrative work himself at a cost of $1500 per week at his hourly rate*

or

B. *He could engage a Virtual Assistant at $35 an hour and together they could identify which parts of the administrative workload could be Delegated to the VA.*

Option B was of course a no-brainer. Dr Kayne was able to reduce his personal administrative workload to 5 hours a week. His VA was initially engaged for 10 hours per week (total spend of $350 per week) which was increased to 15 hours per week as Dr Kayne continued to identify additional tasks he could Delegate to the VA.

Time Reclaimed: 10 hours a week.

This was transformational. Dr Kayne decided to use these reclaimed hours to get his more strategic medical work completed so that he didn't have to work late or, worse, take work home.

Mark this page and return to it to add additional tasks to Delegate as you continue to identify them.

Reframe – SMART Delegation at Home

Many hands make light work — English Proverb

On the home front, Delegates are broken into two categories:

	Definition	What to consider
Delegate – Outsource	The Tasks you currently perform that you would be prepared to pay someone else to do. When you Outsource, you are engaging an expert who will in all likelihood do a much better and quicker job than you.	Keep in mind your Financial Costs: for example, at an hourly rate of $100, four hours of chores at home is $400 of your time. You can engage a Housekeeper for a quarter of that cost. Also keep in mind your Lost Opportunity, Emotional and Physical Costs.

Delegate – Insource	The Tasks you currently do for those you live with that you want them to do for themselves, without pay. Funnily enough, what you may have lost sight of is that you are a partner and/or parent, not a slave.	Keep in mind your Emotional and Physical Costs. Your objective is to ensure your children (and quite possibly your partner) develop into self-sufficient, independent adults.

Outsourcing at Home

> Jack of all trades, master of none
> — English Proverb

Outsourcing is a simple, effective and efficient way to gain back significant hours of time on the home front: reclaimed time you can use to focus on more important tasks. Who wouldn't rather use two hours on a Sunday for a long lunch with friends as opposed to ironing shirts for the week?

What tasks do you currently perform at home that you are now happy to pay someone else to do for you?

EXERCISE 4.2

Outsourcing at Home

Using your Summary Task and Time Spend Table from Exercise 3.2 list every task you have identified as one you can Delegate via outsourcing at home.

When you transfer the data into the table below, group 'like' tasks together and prioritise those tasks that take the greatest amount of your time. Remember, these are the tasks which you will derive a time benefit from outsourcing. It could be that you don't enjoy the task, that it takes too much of your time, or someone else (an expert) can perform the task faster, better and more economically than you. Next work down the Date column and nominate the date (deadline) by which you will have outsourced the task. Keep a running record of the time you reclaim.

Reference Dr Alex's example in the *Doctors Workbook* for additional guidance.

Outsourcing at Home	Date	Time Reclaimed

Example

Dr Kayne next addressed the tasks he was performing on the home front. After completing this exercise, Dr Kayne prioritised cleaning. He was spending 4 hours a week cleaning his house (including clothes washing and ironing) at a cost to him of $400 per week at his hourly rate. It was a big job with lots of hours he could reclaim. Moreover, the Physical and Emotional Costs were a drag. Dr Kayne had a choice:

A.   He could continue to clean his home himself

or

B.   He could engage a cleaner to clean his home.

Not a hard ask. Dr Kayne Delegated (Outsourced) cleaning to a professional who charged him $25 an hour. Being an expert, the cleaner did the job in 3 not 4 hours, at a weekly cost to Dr Kayne of $75. As his second priority, he Outsourced his ironing for $2.00 a shirt, which included the kids' school shirts. Done.

At the end of the day, while the financial outlay to Dr Kayne was low, this wasn't the point. The point was the time he had reclaimed.

Time Reclaimed: 4 hours a week.

Dr Kayne was determined that this reclaimed time wouldn't be absorbed into other chores. He locked in a new rule: every Saturday and Sunday he and the kids would spend 2 hours doing something together. The first Saturday was a bike ride to the park to play some basketball while the first Sunday meant a trip to granddads' for a cup of tea.

Insourcing at Home

Family is a team sport.

The best way to Insource your Delegates at home is to ensure each person you live with is responsible for their own 'stuff'. They are each capable of tidying away their own belongings, hanging up their own wet towels, making their own beds, putting away their own clothes, and so on. Happily, the list of what your family can do for themselves is endless.

There are also any given number of general, family-based, chores that can be done by anyone (and everyone) in your home. For example: taking out the bins, loading and unloading the dishwasher, feeding/cleaning up after/ walking the pets. These types of chores can be divided between household members.

When Insourcing it's important to keep in mind:

1. You are breaking two habits here:

   ⊙ the habits of your family members who are used to leaving their crap lying around because they know you will pick it up and put it away; and

   ⊙ your habit of picking it up and putting it away.

   When there are no clean clothes to wear and they need a map to navigate the journey from their door through their floordrobe to their bed, your kids will eventually get the message.

2. Don't listen to your inner voice who tells you: *It's easier if I just do it myself – it will only take me 5 minutes.* Wrong! While it might initially seem to be easier to do it yourself, it's all about creating independent (not dependent) family members. Besides, it's never just a 5-minute job.

TIP

Add up the minutes:

If you spend 5 minutes every day of the year sorting the dirty washing for your family, that's 30 hours of your time a year.

If you spend 12 minutes every day tidying up all of the crap your kids leave around the house, that's 73 hours of your time a year. That's nearly two working weeks every year!

You get the picture. Your family members are entirely capable of helping around the house. You are establishing new habits for them as well as for yourself. Plus, you are raising strong, independent, capable and helpful (not helpless) individuals.

EXERCISE 4.3

Insourcing at Home

Insourcing will allow you to reclaim a huge number of lost hours. You can see how this can become addictive.

Using your Summary Task and Time Spend Table from Exercise 3.2 prepare a draft Insourcing List. This is just a first cut so you have something to work from when you tackle the Insourcing discussions with the kids. Keep a running record of the time you reclaim.

Reference Dr Alex's example in the *Doctors Workbook* for guidance.

Delegates to Insourced - Daily	Who	Time Reclaimed

Delegates to Insource - Weekly	Who	Time Reclaimed

The best way to finalise your Delegate – Insourcing List is to gain family buy-in.

With your draft List in your pocket as back-up, sit down as a family to discuss what can be Insourced (you already know what you want them to do, but you need them to come up with the list themselves). Your kids are more likely to be, and stay, engaged if they feel they are in control of the process as opposed to being told what they have to do. Let them take the lead on the chores they want to do. Let them write up the Insourcing List on a white board.

To help instil the habit of undertaking chores, start your kids young. When they are little it's all about creating good habits and not so much about getting great results. In all likelihood you will have to remake their beds later when no-one is looking, or re-hang the towel so that it dries, but that's not the point. The point is that you are instilling the right behaviours early. Moreover, the younger your kids are the happier they will be to help. As long as your kids are walking, there are small tasks they can do. Give your 2 year olds their socks to put away.

Example

Dr Kayne was on a roll. After getting a start on Delegates – Outsourcing, he moved on to Delegates – Insourcing. His kids were 8, 10 and 12. Unfortunately he'd been a little inconsistent when it came to making the kids help around the house. Sometimes he was insistent (and then angry and annoyed) and sometimes he was too tired of his own voice and just did the tasks himself. Anything to avoid a fight.

It was time to be consistent. After purchasing a white board he called a family meeting and explained the concept of Insourcing. Family, he said, is a Team Sport. He was happy to mow the lawns, cook three times a week and taxi the kids around to sport. The kids committed to keeping their rooms tidy, putting away their washed clothes, making their beds, changing their linen, sorting their dirty clothes from the clean and making their school lunches. They also agreed to rotate taking out the bins and thought it would be fun to each have a night where they would cook dinner!

Once this was up and running, Dr Kayne found he had to remind the kids of their chores most of the time, but at least the chores got done (by them and not him).

Plus, cooking dinner became an 'all in' task with one person on meat, one on salad/veg, one on dessert, and one on laying the table. After dinner they all cleaned up together. The added bonus here? Dr Kayne started to learn a lot more about what his kids were up to because they actually talked to him while they cooked!

Time Reclaimed: 2 hours a week

Dr Kayne decided to reorganise his Fridays. From now on he would leave work 2 hours early and enjoy some Wants.

Be strong. From now on when you see your family's stuff lying around just begging you to pick it up/clear it away/tidy it/make it magically disappear, take a deep breath, back out of the room and quietly shut the door. Remind your family of what they agreed to do. Who cares if you are the parent who constantly reminds everyone to do their chores? It's better than being the parent who constantly does all of the chores.

> **TIP**
>
> Continually review the Tasks you perform at work and at home to identify what you can Delegate – Outsource and Insource – to harness back even more lost time.

Reframe – Rejects

> Don't bite off more than you can chew
> — American Proverb

Like Delegates, identifying the tasks/habits you can Reject will allow you to reclaim an enormous amount of lost time. Rejects fall into two categories:

Total Rejects	Partial Rejects
The tasks that absolutely no-one needs to do, including you.	The tasks that need to be done, but which can be done much more efficiently.

EXERCISE 4.4

Rejects at Work and Home

Each reader will have a range of behaviours which fall within the definitions of Total Rejects and Partial Rejects, simply because it's just the way you have always done things. Day after day. However, now that you have taken the time in Step 3: Analyse to assess and question the merit of continuing to do the tasks you typically perform, your focus has moved away from *Doing this task (this way) because it's just the way I do it* – to – *Only performing quality tasks because I'm smarter now.*

Using your Summary Task and Time Spend Table from Exercise 3.2, identify each task you currently perform which is a Total Reject and each which is a Partial Reject. Remember, these are the tasks which you will derive an immediate time benefit from by rejecting. When you transfer the data to the table below, group 'like' tasks together and then prioritise the table with those tasks that take the greatest amount of time. For each task, identify the date (deadline) by which you will have Rejected (Total Rejects) or modified (Partial Rejects) the task. Keep a running record of the time you reclaim.

Total Rejects	My Commitment	Date	Time reclaimed per week
Partial Rejects	**My Commitment**		

Start by Rejecting four Tasks (two at work and two at home) that you will gain the biggest amount of time from eliminating from your day. Aim to implement two additional Rejects a week until your current list of Rejects is history. Reference Dr Alex's example for guidance.

> **TIP**
>
> In addition to the tasks you will regain big time wins by Rejecting, don't forget about the low hanging fruit: the tasks or little habits which you know you can easily Reject. Just do it.

Example

Despite the fact that there was another Exercise to complete, Dr Kayne could see the value. He had already reclaimed hours of lost time a week and he knew there was more to be found. He launched into his Rejects Table with gusto!

Dr Kayne's Rejects List

Total Rejects Work	My Commitment	Date	Time reclaimed per week
Piling instead of filing	File immediately, never again start a pile. As much as possible go paperless	12/2	10 mins
Social Media browsing	Don't turn it on to kill time	12/2	30 mins
Keeping email alerts on	Only open emails during allocated email time	14/2	10 mins
Killing time	Keep a list of things to do when I find myself with time	16/2	90 mins
Attending unnecessary meetings	Ask to see the agenda up front; be more selective	12/2	120 mins

Partial Rejects Work	The SMARTER way		
Driving to work listening to the radio	Keep a list of work calls to make	14/2	15 mins
Allowing interruptions	Educate staff on when/ when not to interrupt	20/2	20 mins

Total Rejects Home	My Commitment		Time reclaimed per week
Washing dishes before putting in dishwasher	Never again to pre-wash dishes	12/2	15 mins
Piling instead of filing	File immediately, never again start a pile	12/2	2 mins
Face-to-face banking	Go online and set up auto pay	19/2	5 mins
Social Media browsing	Put the device in the study and stay away from it	12/2	85 mins
Cleaning before the cleaner comes	The cleaner has seen worse, surely	12/2	20 mins

Partial Rejects Home	The SMARTER way		
Supermarket most days	Make a weekly Meal Plan and then shop once (online!)	16/2	30 mins
Deciding on the day what I will make for dinner	Meal Plan	16/2	35 mins
Cooking every night (3 nights a week)	Cook double batches and freeze half for another night	16/2	60 mins
Washing the bath towels every day	Once a week is fine	20/2	15 mins

TIP

There is absolutely no excuse for continuing to do the tasks you have identified as Rejects. However, some of your Rejects will take a little time to sort out. The best way to manage this is to schedule a block of time into your Calendar to set yourself up for success. For example, allocate 3 hours next Friday afternoon to go through unsubscribing from junk emailed newsletters, cancelling journals you don't read, subscribing to an online shopping account, setting up your weekly shopping list and so on. This is a once-off job so suck it up.

Print out your Rejects List, keep it close and lock a date in your Calendar to reflect on your progress in 2 weeks time. You are establishing new habits (remember, 6 weeks of repetition), so you need to keep yourself accountable.

Continually review the tasks you perform at work and at home to identify new Rejects or to address old habits which may have crept back in unnoticed.

Reframe – Your Wants

This is where you get to identify all the awesome things you Want to do with the hours you have reclaimed. The very reason you want to manage your time as effectively as possible is to maximise the number of hours you have available for the things you love to do. Your Wants are otherwise known as *Me Time*, just in case that's a concept you have never given consideration to.

EXERCISE 4.5

It's all about my Wants

You have a draft Wants List you created in Step 1: Self-Aware (and it's pinned to your wall). While working through *The 5 SMART Steps* other possibilities will have opened up to you; new ideas of what to do with your time now that you have started regaining control of your time.

Using your Summary Task and Time Spend Table from Exercise 3.2 along with your draft Wants List from Exercise 1.5, update your Wants List below. Identify the priority of each Want and the date (deadline) by which you will have started enjoying the Want.

My Wants List

Wants	Priority	Date

Next, re-write your Wants List on a new piece of paper in priority order and match each Want with a corresponding Core Value(s). Why? Because this is not an ad hoc wish list of random dreams. It's a well thought out Wants List which has its origin from your inner-most drivers. It's validating to link your Wants back to your Core Values.

Example

Dr Kayne had been tracking his reclaimed time and had already locked in his highest priority Wants. But there was more to be had:

Wants	Priority	Core Value	Date
2 hours Saturday doing indoor fun 'stuff' with the kids	#1	Family Time	Done!
2 hours Sunday doing outdoor fun 'stuff' with the kids	#2	Family Time	Done!
3 hours a week at the gym	#3	Healthy	Monday
3 hours cooking/baking class with the kids	#4	Family Time	Next intake
3 hours additional work opportunities	#5	Professional	Friday

TIP

Schedule your Wants into your Calendar and make sure you turn up. You wouldn't just 'not turn up' to an appointment with your Accountant or your own Doctor, so treat yourself with the same level of respect.

Continually revisit your Wants List. There is nothing you can't do!

Stay committed. Don't let your Musts, Delegates and Rejects encroach on the time you allocate to your Wants.

Checklist: Now You Know

- [ ] What (and by when) you will Delegate at work.
- [ ] What (and by when) you will Delegate (Outsource) at home.
- [ ] What (and by when) you will Delegate (Insource) at home.
- [ ] What (and by when) you will Reject (Total and Partial) at home.
- [ ] What (and by when) you will Reject (Total and Partial) at work.
- [ ] What (and by when) you will implement your Wants.

It's time to Take Action.

Step 5

TAKE ACTION

*All things are difficult before they
are easy — Chinese Proverb*

You have completed the first four steps of *The 5 SMART Steps* and have identified exactly what you plan to Delegate and Reject to harness hours of lost time. You have also identified where you are going to spend the time you reclaim. What you need now is to Take Action to ensure you implement the changes you have identified.

Step 5: Take Action is where you turn the theory learnt and the data collected in the first four steps into Actions (new time management habits) you can implement to realise and then sustain massive time savings.

At the end of Step 5: Take Action you will have:

⊙ an Action Plan which consolidates in one place the Actions you identified in Step 4: Reframe.

⊙ commenced implementing your Actions

Simple is best. Set up your Action Plan to maximise your success. A complex Action Plan with too much detail and too many layers will set you up for failure. Besides, what a waste of time!

EXERCISE 5.1

My Action Plan

Refer back to the Exercises in Step 4: Reframe and transcribe as an Action the activities you have identified as Delegates (work and home) and Rejects (work and home) into the Action Plan below (or in your *Doctors Workbook*). Note the deadline, lock the deadline into your Calendar, then complete each Action by your identified deadline. Keep a running record of the time you reclaim to be allocated to your Wants.

You need to keep yourself accountable; you have come this far, it's time to implement. Refer to Dr Alex's example in the *Doctors Workbook* for additional guidance.

> **TIP**
>
> When you fill in your Action Plan, make sure that your deadlines are realistic and achievable. If you are overly ambitious with the proposed dates you nominated in Step 4: Reframe, you may need to adjust now.
>
> Your best sequence is to discard your Total Rejects immediately - *today!* - and your Partial Rejects soon after. Those were simple wins and will help free up time for you to address your Delegates.

Action Plan	Date	Action Completed	Time Reclaimed
Delegates at Work			
Delegates Outsourced at Home			
Delegates Insourced at Home			
Total Rejects at Work			
Partial Rejects at Work			

Action Plan	Date	Action Completed	Time Reclaimed

Total Rejects at Home

| | | | |

Partial Rejects at Home

| | | | |

Total Time Reclaimed

What are you waiting for? Come on - do it! Start right now! Go go go!

For every 1 hour you reclaim grab your Wants list from the wall and choose a Want to commence immediately. Remember, 1 hour reclaimed = 1 hour to spend on a Want!

Congratulations!

You have completed *The 5 SMART Steps*!

TIP

Email me at success@timestylers.com when you have implemented enough Actions to have added 4 hours every week to your Want List. In your email, list some of the tasks you have Delegated and Rejected, and list some of the Wants you have implemented. I will reply back with some additional content as a Bonus!

The 5 SMART Steps is an iterative process. You now know what you are doing and can continue to revisit your Musts, Wants, Delegates and Rejects to maintain your momentum. You will also need to revisit *The 5 SMART Steps* as your life circumstances change.

What's Next?

You have completed *The 5 SMART Steps* and you have implemented your Action Plan. If you need additional assistance in implementation, use the following timeframe as a general guide.

Let's recap. This is what you have already done:

Step	Timeframe
Step 1: Self-Aware	
Your Key Time Management Challenges	Week 1
Your Core Values: those values which guide the decisions you make and where you choose to spend your time	Week 1
The need to integrate all aspects of your life	Week 1
Step 2: Map	
The tasks you undertook across 3 Typical days	Week 2
What a Better Day would (and is about to) look like	Week 2
Step 3: Analyse	
The tasks you Must perform	Week 2-3
The tasks you Want to perform	Week 2-3
The tasks you could Delegate	Week 2-3
The tasks you could Reject	Week 2-3
The costs associated with how you have been spending your time: Financial, Lost Opportunity, Emotional and Physical	Week 4

Step 4: Reframe

Exactly what you are going to Delegate	Week 5
Exactly what you are going to Reject	Week 5
Your growing list of Wants	Week 5
Keep track of your reclaimed time	Week 5

Step 5: Take Action

Establish your Action Plan	Week 6
Complete your Action Plan	Week 6–9
Lock your Wants into your Calendar	Week 6-9 and ongoing

From Week 6-9 and ongoing, focus on settling in the new habits you have committed to in your Action Plan. Keep an eye on what is working well and what needs ongoing self-discipline.

Keep a record of the hours you reclaim each week and make sure you lock into your Calendar a corresponding Want for the same amount of reclaimed time. Remember, the whole idea of *The 5 SMART Steps* is to use your reclaimed hours to do what you love most.

When you have reclaimed 4 hours a week (and you know there is more to be gained), it's time for you to up the ante. Return to Part B for some proven productivity strategies to supercharge your time management.

PART B

....

Supercharge Your Productivity with the Control Framework

Bad habits are easier to abandon today
than tomorrow — Yiddish Proverb

The Control Framework

You have completed *The 5 SMART Steps*, including implementing your Action Plan. You have reclaimed hours of lost time to spend on your Wants. The question is, can you do even better?

Sure you can.

> **TIP**
>
> Discarding old habits and embedding new habits takes time and work. You know this. It takes 6 weeks to genuinely lock in a new habit such that it becomes second nature.
>
> You want to maximise your success, so don't commence Part B until 12 weeks after you started reading this book.

In Part B you will be exposed to a range of strategies (aka further new habits and behaviours) you can implement to supercharge your productivity.

Let's Do It!

You still have a general routine you follow each day (get up, get to work, buy coffee, see first patient …). This routine is supplemented by a mental *To Do List*. You may occasionally or even routinely render your To Do List to writing, but generally speaking you know what you need to get done. Unfortunately, there are tasks which either fall into the *Too Hard Basket* or which fall through the cracks.

Equally, you have a calendar which you may use quite well or which you may use sporadically. However more often than not you have multiple calendars which require some effort to cross reference (and so you don't) or you choose to function from your clinic calendar and generally wing the rest. Should a cancellation arise you rarely take advantage of the free 15 minutes you just reclaimed as you don't have a back-up plan to ensure you use all of your time well. Besides, you reason, what's the point in starting something new when you only have 15 minutes?

Most days you put your head down and get your work done. However, you would love to be able to better focus on the task at hand for longer periods of time, to say *No* to the requests you wish you hadn't said *Yes* to, and to tactfully manage interruptions.

Sound familiar? If so, it's time to Control the agenda to supercharge your productivity.

The Control Framework

In Step 1: Self-Aware (Exercise 1.2) you identified your three Key Time Management Challenges. These could cover myriad issues depending on the demands on your time and your current time management skills. Regardless of what you identified, the vast majority of time management challenges doctors experience are associated with a lack of control.

In order to Control your time, you need to Control your Clarity, Control your Calendar and Control your Commitment. Each of these elements is connected. This is called the Control Framework.

When you master the Control Framework you will master your time management.

TIP

Minimise the amount of your day that is dictated to you by the agendas of those around you. This may seem easier said than done, particularly if you are lower down in the pecking order at work. However, regardless of your level of seniority, or the degree to which your job is driven by reactive rather than proactive drivers, you will have a base level of Control over your own agenda which you may not be leveraging to its full extent.

In short, you need to identify what you do have Control over, whether this is 1%, 10% or 100% of your daily activities, and you need to seize that Control.

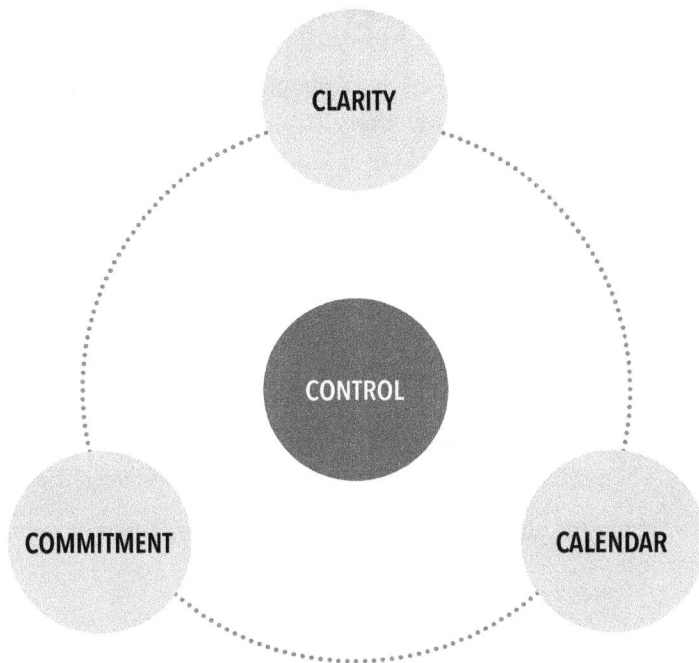

There are a wide range of proven strategies I use to supercharge my clients' productivity, some of which are presented here in Part B and segmented under the three elements of the Control Framework: Clarity, Calendar and Commitment.

As each element of the Control Framework interacts with the other elements, you will maximise your time management efficiencies by implementing productivity strategies from each of the three elements: **the right level of Clarity in conjunction with the best use of your Calendar will ensure your Commitment to using all of your time well.**

How to Use Part B

As you consider which productivity strategies to implement from Part B, start with the low-hanging fruit: those strategies where you automatically think *Why didn't I think of that?* Once you have the no-brainers locked in, select the strategies which you can see will make a significant difference to how you currently manage your time. The whole idea is to regain even more lost time to spend on what you most love. Where you can take an Action(s) to implement a new strategy, you will see this Icon:

The more productivity strategies you implement from Part B and then sustain, the better Control you will have over your time management.

When you master the Control Framework you will master your time management.

Control – Element 1: Clarity

Planning is half of living — Arabic Proverb

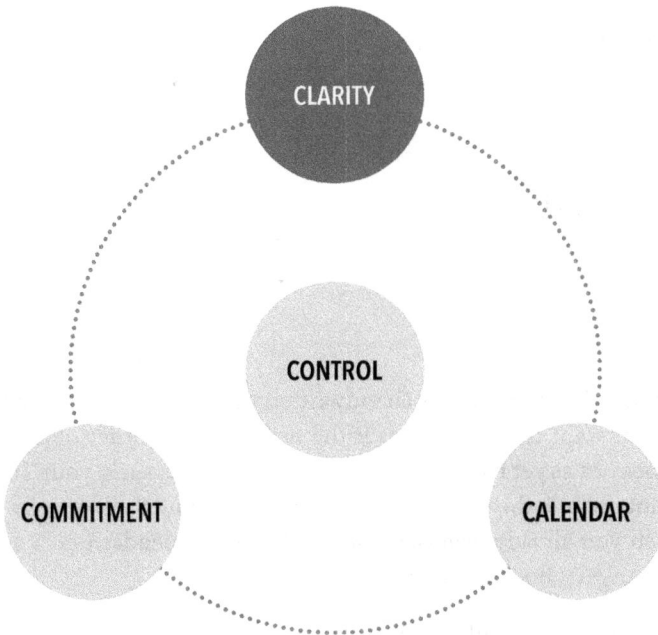

What is Element 1: Clarity?

Clarity – or absolute certainty of purpose – means knowing exactly what you want to achieve and exactly the steps you need to take in order of importance, to get there. Having maximum Clarity over your work and life roles, goals and plans – and then executing on these – is critical to ensuring you spend your *Best Time* on the right tasks.

How do I use Clarity?

The Clarity element of the Control Framework includes establishing the right strategies to ensure you know exactly the tasks (work and home) you have on your plate, how long each task will take, by when each task must be delivered, and the importance and hence priority of each task.

You can gain and maintain Clarity with a number of productivity tools and strategies.

Clarity Strategies

Clarity – Your To Do List

> The palest ink is better than the best memory.
> — Chinese Proverb

A To Do List is a transcribed (handwritten or electronic) list of every task you need or want to complete over the next week, in order of priority, but which does not as yet have an immediate deadline. As such, your To Do List should not include the tasks which are the very foundation of your Practice and which you already have scheduled into your calendar (such as patient consults, surgery, hospital rounds).

If you have been subsisting with a mental To Do List you are definitely not operating with maximum Clarity. Tasks will have been forgotten or will have fallen through the cracks. Moreover, you will have limited ability to accurately weigh up the competing value of multiple tasks in order to prioritise tasks.

Each Sunday night spend 10 minutes on a brain dump of the tasks which must be completed in the coming week at both work and home (but which, as noted above, are not already in your Calendar). This is your master To Do List which you will revisit each night.

The following Key Tasks should be included in your To Do List:

Example

Key Task	Examples
Work	Meetings, strategic tasks, business planning, research papers, time each evening to update your To Do List
Events	Birthdays, anniversaries, holidays, kids sports days
Regulatory/ Compliance	Tax, insurance, registration, memberships
Study	CPD, classes, teaching commitments, journal reading
Personal	Dentist, school engagements, social engagements, meeting experts to undertake your identified Outsource activities, breaks between chunks of work, time for your Wants

Identify your Top 3 Key Tasks in order of priority for Monday and estimate how long each Key Task will take. Your Time Sheets (Step 2: Map) will give you a good idea of how long such tasks generally take. It is important that you allocate an appropriate and realistic time estimate to each Key Task, otherwise your day could be thrown out by a task you have significantly under-estimated and you will find yourself playing catch-up.

TIP

Since Mapping your time, you already know when you are most energised and when you are not.

Your *Best Time* is your daily high energy point (and when you are most creative, enthusiastic and impactful). This time must be respected and devoted entirely to your Hairiest Task.

Your *Hairiest Task* is your most strategically important, difficult, challenging task each day which will return the highest results.

Include in your To Do List any tasks you need to start to ensure you meet a deadline in a few weeks time. You need to do this so that you are not caught out by a task which was looming but you didn't have time to address.

A task with a vague or arbitrary deadline is not a Key Task and should remain on your To Do List until such time as you have assigned it a specific deadline.

> **TIP**
>
> Learn as you go. If you have been allocating 20 minutes on your To Do List to a task and yet your Time Sheets indicate that the task actually takes closer to 30 minutes, then adjust going forward.

Delete or cross out each activity you complete on your To Do List because it looks great and it will keep you motivated.

Each evening spend 10 minutes re-visiting your master To Do List for the next day to identify:

- ⊙ your Top 3 Key Tasks, and of these your Hairiest Task
- ⊙ any new tasks which need to be accommodated
- ⊙ if your time estimates are accurate
- ⊙ any long-term deliverables
- ⊙ completed tasks which can be deleted from your To Do List.

> **TIP**
>
> Go to www.timestylers.com to access and print out the template To Do List, or source a To Do List that works for you. Schedule time into your Calendar for the next six Sunday nights, and then each night of the week in between, to keep you accountable until such time as maintaining your new To Do List becomes a habit.

A sample of the Time Stylers To Do List is shown below:

Daily To Do List (T̄S) **Time Stylers**

DAILY TO DO LIST	PRIORITY	TIME

What would you do with 30 extra hours a month?

www.timestylers.com

Remember to add tasks from your Wants List to your To Do List.

Clarity – Your Deadlines

What may be done at any time will be done at no time
— Scottish Proverb

A Deadline is the time you set for having a task, or part of a task, completed. A task will only remain on your To Do List until you set a Deadline for its completion. Setting realistic but hard Deadlines will keep you on task and will minimise time wastage.

In this regard, think Parkinson's Law: the notion that work expands to fill the time available for its completion. By way of example:

Example

If you have a 3-hour window in which to update ten patient records, the task will take you 3 hours. However, if you have a 4-hour window, then the task will expand to fill 4 hours.

That's Parkinson's Law.

Referencing your Time Sheets, set a realistic Deadline for each Key Task on your To Do List. In terms of being realistic, this one is common sense:

◉ If the Deadline is remarkably too short then you are setting yourself up for panic and failure.

◉ If the Deadline is remarkably too generous then you are setting yourself up for procrastination and failure.

Keep an eye on your To Do List time estimates (see the far right-hand column in the sample To Do List above). If your time estimates are too tight, adjust them to ensure you set yourself up for success.

As you gain confidence that your task time estimates are accurate, then leverage Parkinson's Law to ensure you are operating at maximum efficiency. You can do this by closely monitoring how long a task generally takes (from your Time Sheets) and then challenge yourself to undertake the task in less time. Tighten the screws a little each time you perform the activity until you reach the sweet point of maximum efficiency: the best possible result in the most efficient timeframe.

> **TIP**
>
> Keep an eye on the tasks you regularly park until later or which seem to permanently reside in the *Too Hard Basket*. If they are mundane process-driven tasks, lock in a Deadline and schedule it into your Calendar. Similarly, if you are procrastinating over a complex task, identify it as a Key Task, schedule a Deadline and lock it into your Calendar.

Example

Dr Susan writes a monthly blog post of 700 words for a Medical Journal which gives her great credibility. She was in the habit of leaving this task until the last minute and even then she would stop and start the job multiple times which led to a lot of re-work. After monitoring her Time Sheets (Step 2: Map), Dr Susan found that in total the task generally took 4 hours to complete over 2–3 days.

In the first instance, Dr Susan used Parkinson's Law to allocate 4 hours a month to write her blog and scheduled a hard Deadline in her Calendar.

Her next step was to leverage Parkinson's Law. She set herself the goal of writing the blog in two sittings of an hour each. This hard Deadline was locked into her Calendar. A big challenge compared to her old habit!

Dr Susan found a quiet place to work where she would not be interrupted and she turned her phone off to eliminate distractions. She got completely ready with water and music to stop herself getting up and down and generally procrastinating once the task started. She set a timer for an hour and achieved a solid draft that she was happy with.

Two days later Dr Susan repeated this process and she finalised the blog post in 40 minutes.

Month on month, Dr Susan challenged herself to deliver the blog more and more efficiently. Ultimately she established the discipline of completing the blog post in one sitting of 1 hour.

By doing so, she reclaimed 3 hours a month; that's 3 hours which she scheduled into her Calendar to spend on her next Want (surf lessons down the coast!).

Count all of your reclaimed minutes as they come back to you. Use all of this reclaimed time well by scheduling time in your Calendar for your Wants.

TIP

Time three typical tasks to ascertain how long they generally take. Lock these tasks into your Calendar as a Deadline to ensure you establish the discipline of always working to these timeframes. Next, leverage Parkinson's Law and tighten the timeframes a few minutes at a time – continually measuring your results – until you reach the sweet point of maximum efficiency. Next, move on to your next three tasks and so on.

Example

An average patient consult took Dr Chris 21 minutes. As he saw 20 patients a day, this totalled 7 hours of consulting time each day.

At its simplest, Dr Chris used Parkinson's Law and asked his Practice Manager to allocate 21 minutes to each patient.

Next, Dr Chris leveraged Parkinson's Law and set himself the goal of reducing each consult time to an average of 18 minutes. This would allow him to reduce his consulting time to 6 hours a day. Dr Chris was comfortable that a 3-minute time reduction per patient would not compromise patient care.

As a control measure, Dr Chris asked his Practice Manager to time the appointments over a period of 3 days. Together, they were able to reclaim an hour of Dr Chris' time each day.

Dr Chris kept track of his reclaimed time and scheduled this time in his Calendar with the intent of leaving work early once a week to play golf.

Checklist: Now You Know

You can gain greater Clarity over your time with productivity tools and strategies such as:

☐   To Do Lists

☐   Deadlines

☐   Parkinson's Law

It's time to work on your Calendar.

Control – Element 2: Calendar

Man who waits for roast duck to fly into his mouth must wait a very, very long time — Chinese Proverb

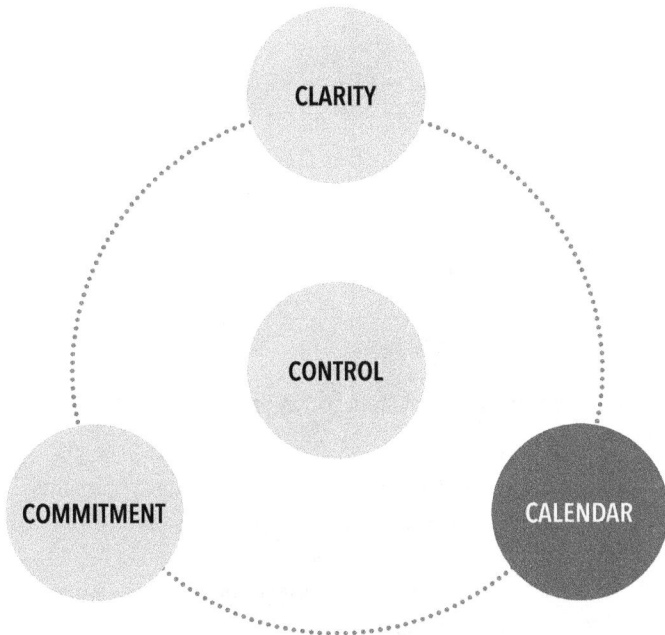

What is Element 2: Calendar?

The ongoing and disciplined management of your Calendar in conjunction with having true Clarity over your work and ensuring your Commitment to undertake the right task at the right time will help you Take Control of your time.

The main difference between your Calendar and your To Do List is that your Calendar only includes the Key Tasks which have a Deadline. Together, your To Do List and Calendar are a powerful time management team.

How do I use my Calendar?

If you are currently managing multiple Calendars (for example: Practice/ Appointments Calendar, Personal Work Calendar, Social Calendar, Family Calendar) you are not only wasting time juggling and cross-referencing your various engagements, but there are simply too many moving parts to allow you to use all of your time well. Remember: simple is best.

Calendar Strategies

Undertake now to run all of your Key Tasks (both work and home) from one Calendar so that your Calendar operates as a true reflection of your total time commitment. By having everything in one place you will have absolute Control over your time and nothing will fall through the cracks.

> **TIP**
>
> If you don't have support staff, focus on only one Calendar which covers:
>
> ▸ your general/day-to-day patient appointments/consults
> ▸ work tasks that sit outside your general appointments/consults
> ▸ study tasks
> ▸ non-work life tasks including celebrations, family events, sports, holidays, get-togethers, appointments
> ▸ family responsibilities.
>
> If you have an Assistant/Practice Manager/Receptionist, they will be responsible for setting and maintaining your general/day-to-day patient appointments/consults from a Practice Calendar.

You can focus on only one Calendar which is synced to the Practice Calendar so you know what gaps you have in your schedule to accommodate the following:

▶ work tasks that sit outside your general appointments/consults
▶ study tasks
▶ non-work tasks including celebrations, family events, sports, holidays, get-togethers, appointments
▶ family responsibilities.

Once you have identified your Key Tasks from your To Do List and have allocated Deadlines to these tasks, lock the tasks into your Calendar immediately. This allows you to ascertain at a glance what your day/week/month looks like, as well as the time that is available for other tasks from your To Do List (including your Wants).

Include all relevant information in your Calendar for each Key Task. For example, if you have a conference call scheduled in your Calendar, also include the telephone number in the Calendar entry so that you don't waste 10 minutes at a later date trawling through your Inbox looking for the caller's contact details.

The disciplined use of your Calendar will reduce the chances of: procrastination (*um … what should I do next?*), forgetting a task, trying to be in two or more places at once, and allowing distractions or unscheduled interruptions. Moreover, by scheduling a Deadline for each Key Task, your Calendar will help you maintain your Commitment to focus on one task at a time. You will work through your tasks more efficiently and move on to the next scheduled task with less wasted time.

Setting up an online Calendar via the Cloud will provide you with a real time view of your schedule and is accessible by any device within your Control. Understand and leverage the functionality of your online Calendar. This will not only save you a massive amount of time, but it will literally change the way you work.

Example

Calendar Feature	Benefit
Categorise your Calendar	Moving from a one page/category view to multiple category views can be as simple as colour coding or adding icons to each different type of Key Task. For example, Events can be coloured Blue while Regulatory/Compliance can be coloured Red and so on. Having all aspects of your life in one categorised Calendar makes for a less complicated system and provides a simple way to quickly identify and juggle all of your commitments in one place. You can view your Calendar as a whole (all Key Tasks) or just one category at a time (e.g. Personal Appointments).
Sync your Calendar with your email	Allows you to schedule Key Tasks directly from your email.
Sync your Calendar with your team	Allows you to plan Key Tasks involving others according to the attendees' schedules, eliminating back and forth communications. Colleagues can readily identify when you are and are not available.
Sync Calendars with your partner	Additions you both make will be updated across both Calendars. Your partner can readily identify when you are and are not available. You can readily identify when your partner is and is not available.
Include Attachments	Allows you to easily access relevant documents/details directly from your Calendar, saving the time it normally takes to find what you need in your Inbox (generally 3 minutes before the meeting starts!)
Recurring activities	Identify and lock-in recurring tasks such as team meetings, birthdays and anniversaries across the year. This will save a lot of time each week in planning your upcoming week. For birthdays and anniversaries, set a Reminder 1-week out so you have time to buy present, card, write in the card, wrap present and make a restaurant reservation.

Each Sunday night and then each evening when you prepare your To Do List, lock your Key Tasks into your Calendar and remove/delete/cross out the task from your To Do List. Once you have established the daily discipline of these Calendar Basics, move on to Calendar Batching.

What is Calendar Batching?

Batching is the process of grouping like tasks together and then blocking out slabs of time in your Calendar to complete these tasks in one larger chunk of time. Batching allows you to have one longer, concentrated period of time allocated to dealing with, for example, emails in bulk, as opposed to jumping in and out of your email repeatedly throughout the day. You end up with one clean and structured Calendar, and an uncluttered mind, as opposed to having a hectic and disorganised day.

In addition, by Batching 'like' tasks together in your Calendar you can operate *in the zone* for a longer period of time, ensuring you maintain your focus. Working for a dedicated period of time on like tasks also gives you greater Control over the time it takes you to transition from one task to the next, reducing the margin for error that comes with jumping in and out of tasks.

How do I use Calendar Batching?

From your Time Sheets and your recent close observation of how, when and where you are spending your time, you are well placed to set your Calendar up to ensure maximum productivity. Batching can be used in many ways including:

Batching Strategies

Batch – Your Best Time

Refer back to Exercise 2.2 and note the time of the day which is your *Best Time* (that is, the time of day when you are at your highest energy point and hence most creative, enthusiastic and impactful). It is critical to spend your *Best Time* in the right place and on the right, or *Hairiest*, Task (that is, your most strategically important, difficult, challenging task which will return the highest results).

In your Calendar, block out 45–60 minutes of your *Best Time* for your Hairiest Task as identified in your To Do List.

Do not waste your *Best Time* on anything less.

Take a 5–10 minute break and then, knowing whether you are still within a high energy period, block out another Batch of time to continue with your Hairiest Task or move to your next Task.

> **TIP**
>
> If you are a dynamo early in the morning, you will be full of energy at 6am and ready to jump into the day. Don't waste this time on checking emails or reading the paper. Instead, Batch your *Best Time* into your Calendar to deal with your Hairiest Task for the day: the task that is complicated or requires uninterrupted and focussed thinking.

Great uses of your *Best Time* include business planning, writing a report on a complex case, studying for an exam or preparing a paper for an upcoming conference.

Batch - Your lowest energy ebb

Refer back to Exercise 2.2, and look at when you are at your lowest energy ebb. Block this time in your Calendar for a Batch of the more mundane, low risk, process-driven work that does not require as much concentration or thought.

Example

Dr Monty found that each Friday afternoon his team were literally limping to the finish line. He decided to implement a Friday Process Batch from 3.30pm-4.30pm. He encouraged the team to complete easy, process-driven tasks such as finalising the filing, ordering stationery and decluttering their desks. Without question it was a more relaxing way to end the week, with staff heading home stress free and arriving back on Monday morning to an ordered office, ready for a fresh start.

Batch Compliance and Regulatory tasks

It can be hard to think of a more heavily regulated industry than that of healthcare. You are operating in an industry with complex schemes overseen by an array of regulatory bodies covering practising medicine, medical registration, dispensing of medication, reporting responsibilities, record keeping, insurance, keeping memberships up to date, disclosing conflicts of interest, medical indemnity reporting, medical devices, complementary medicine and so on. The vast majority of these regulations are not one-off requirements, with many requiring at least annual compliance.

Batch - Build in time for the unexpected

> The donkey does not bump into the same stone twice
> — Dutch Proverb

A useful Batching strategy is to block breathing space into your Calendar. Working in the medical profession you will be well aware that not all days run smoothly. Factor in the possibility that you may need to dedicate time to something unpredictable. You can do this by blocking out a 30–40 minute period each day for the unexpected. If nothing unexpected arises, use this time for a Want or move on to the next item on your To Do List. If something unexpected does come up, you can shuffle the rest of your day accordingly knowing that you have a built in 30–40 minute buffer.

Batch Device Management - General

> Good habits result from resisting
> temptation — Indian Proverb

The average smartphone user checks their phone 85 times a day and more than half these instances last less than 30 seconds. Not good for productivity. Take Control of your device usage with Batching.

Think about a typical day. The alarm goes off, you wake and stretch, you roll out of bed to go to the toilet and … you reach for your smartphone. You know you do this. When was the last time you let a work day pass without checking your phone? Too hard? OK, when was the last time you spent two phone/email/text-free hours?

When you start your day on your device, particularly on email (think the 6am quick check of your phone), and then continue to glance and review emails and text messages regularly throughout the day, you are operating in a reactive rather than a proactive way. You are basically working to someone else's agenda.

Device usage is not all bad. A smartphone is an essential tool for the modern doctor. As a work-related tool your device can significantly reduce the amount of time many tasks would otherwise take. However, the constant compulsion to check your device coupled with using your device as a *time killer* (such as checking social media) can severely impact your ability to use all of your time well. Moreover, the proliferation of portable devices affords you constant exposure to your emails, texts, messages and social media alerts which, unchecked, allows for an incessant stream of interruptions, decreased productivity and loss of focus.

If you are prone to jumping on and off your phone every time you hear that lovely little *ping,* feel a vibration, or see an alert flash on your screen, then your device may have turned from friend to foe.

Most people considerably under-estimate the amount of time they spend on their smartphone and other devices. To get an accurate picture of your own device usage and the Financial Cost of this, refer to your Time Sheets (Step 2: Map) and your hourly rate (Step 3: Analyse) and complete the table below.

There is an example below in italics:

Activity	Hours over 7 days x 52 weeks x hourly rate	Your calculations
My smartphone usage (checking emails, text messages, taking/making calls, social media)	*7 hours x 52 x $100 = $36,400*	

My office computer usage (checking emails, social media) on workdays	*5 hours x 52 x $100 = $26,000*
	Total = $62,400

Of course, this is a great investment of your time if you are being productive and using your device as a value-adding business tool. However, it is more likely that your device and associated email checking have become the Mother of All Distractions. If the latter, then it's time to count the costs and make the necessary adjustments.

The reason you Batch device usage – particularly the management of emails and calls – is to ensure you Control your time. Batching allows you to choose when and where it makes most sense for you to check your emails, messages, and make or return calls.

In your Calendar, schedule email/call/text management into three or four discrete Batches across the day. Schedule the first Batch for the 30–40 minutes immediately following the 5–10 minute break you take after your Hairiest Task.

> **TIP**
>
> Schedule 3 x 30 minute Device Batches at 10am, 12 noon and 4pm. Between each Batch turn your alerts off (visual and auditory) so that you aren't distracted or tempted to multitask. Where possible, and if you aren't on-call, turn your phone off between Batches.

If you find the early morning email/device addiction hard to break, don't give up. Rather, employ the above technique with a one day on/one day off approach. For the day that you are 'off' (that is, not following the strategy), monitor the incoming traffic and assess how many genuinely urgent emails or messages you receive. Consider also whether patient care or the running of your Practice could have been compromised by the hour's delay. Remember, if something is genuinely urgent, you can be reached by a pager alert.

Batch Device Management - Emails

Once you have the hang of dealing with your emails in discrete Batches, you can triage your Inbox with the 4 D's in mind:

Email Triage Table

Triage	Action
Deal with it	Emails concerning a matter of high impact/urgency should be addressed first in each Email Batch. Flag them Red.
Defer it	Emails requiring a considered response or some thinking time should be parked for a later scheduled Email Batch to let your subconscious work on it. Flag them Yellow.
	But first, send a quick response along the lines of: *I have received your email and will come back to you by <date/time>*. That way the sender won't continue to chase you.
Delegate it	Emails which can be dealt with by someone else on your team, such as your Practice Manager, should be delegated and removed from your Inbox.
Delete it	Emails you can Reject/immediately delete include spam, junk or subscriptions you no longer want to receive.
	Unsubscribe from unwanted subscriptions prior to deletion.

Batch Device Management – Calls

Habit is second nature — Latin Proverb

You can also triage which phone calls you return using the same Triage strategy as above. Just substitute the concept of 'Email' with 'Return Phone Calls'.

Further, because phone calls require real-time 1:1 interaction with another person (unlike emails), you can employ additional strategies to deal with calls in a timely manner. Take the following scenarios for example:

Example

You can gain considerable control over the time you spend on phone calls by recording and leaving meaningful messages which provide clear instructions to callers and set their expectations as to how and when you will respond, such as:

Hi, it's Dana, leave a brief message to let me know how I can help you. I check my messages periodically each day and will respond to you either by phone, text or email. If the matter is urgent then please …

Or

Hi, It's Dana. I'm sorry I can't take your call, however the quickest way to reach me is via text …

Example

During an Email/Phone Batch when you initiate a call, Take Control of the conversation by framing the amount of time you have, such as:

Hi Sally, it's Dana, I have 10 minutes before my next consult and …

Example

When you make a call and the person is not there, respect their time and set your future exchange up for success and good time management by leaving a meaningful message.

Don't say: Hi, it's Dana, please call me back. This is vague and provides the recipient with no information to help them help you.

Rather leave clear instructions: Hi, it's Dana, please call me back to let me know what medication is required for patient Daphne Smith.

Example

Where possible turn your phone off and return calls in a Phone Batch. However, if you need to leave your phone on and take incoming calls, then Take Control of the conversation.

Do not ask: Hi, how are you? as this is an invitation for the person to tell you how they actually are. It sounds antisocial, but really, unless it's your mum do you really care how the caller is? You are inviting 10 minutes of lost time.

Instead, try: It's good to hear from you. How can I help you? If the answer is a rambling laundry list of issues, politely interrupt with I'm just walking into a meeting. Send me an email/ text setting out in dot points exactly how I can help.

Once you have the hang of Batching, you will start to see Batching opportunities everywhere.

Embrace Batching and schedule blocks of time into your Calendar for the tasks identified above. Other tasks you can Batch include:

- Patient consultations/ward rounds
- Home-based tasks (cleaning, bill paying, shopping, errands, cooking)
- Study
- Reading/Continuing Professional Development
- Medical billing
- Sending your tax information to your Accountant.

Checklist: Now You Know

Leverage your Calendar with SMART Time Management strategies including:

- ☐ Use one Calendar for everything
- ☐ Utilise an Online Calendar
- ☐ All things Batching

It's time to work on your Commitment.

Control – Element 3: Commitment

If you do not enter the tiger's cave you will not catch its cubs — Japanese Proverb

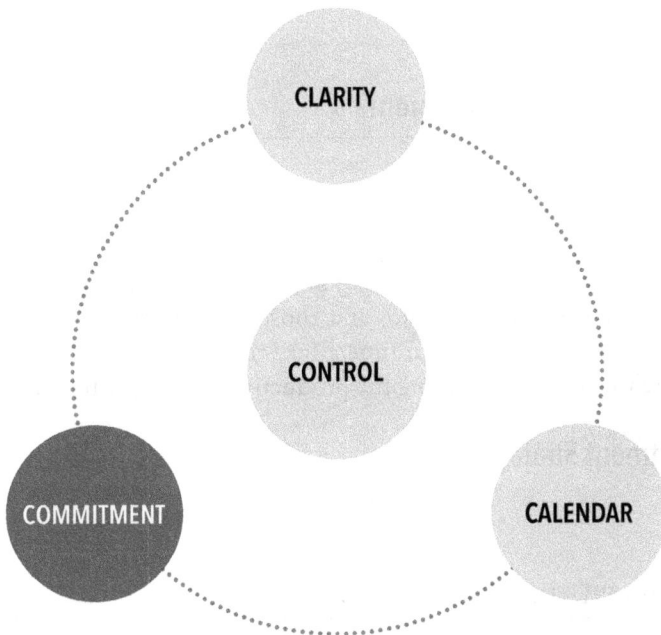

What is Element 3: Commitment?

Commitment is focus; focus on performing the right tasks at the right time until completion.

We live in the Age of Information, which also means we live in the Age of Distraction. The average attention span is 8 seconds (less than the common goldfish, which is believed to have an attention span of 9 seconds). This means that the average attention span switches from the task at hand to something else or back again seven times every minute. Recognising this, modern doctors need some specific behaviours and habits to maximise their Commitment and maintain their focus.

Are you still with me? Sorry, couldn't resist.

> **TIP**
>
> Make a Commitment to each new habit. Then do it again, and again, and again. And then again. For 6 weeks. It will soon become your way of doing things.

How do I employ Commitment?

Repetition teaches even a donkey
— Arabic Proverb

Since Step 2: Map and Step 3: Analyse you have a very good sense of the behaviours and habits you hold, and those you tolerate in others, which impact the effective use of your time. Make the Commitment to using all of your time well by implementing the productivity strategies below.

Commitment Strategies

Commitment – use your Lost Time

Every mikkle meek a mukkle (Every bit counts)
— Jamaican Proverb

Everyone has *Lost Time* that they don't take full advantage of. By identifying and harnessing your Lost Time, not only will you get through many of the small tasks that you often don't reach, but you will also maintain a high level of efficiency by using all of your time well.

From your Time Sheets and generally reflecting on how your days pan out, you will see that periodically throughout each day there are small periods of unexpected or unplanned downtime. For example, a patient may not turn up for a 15-minute appointment without notice; your walk between your office and hospital rounds provides a 10-minute period; you are stuck in traffic for 15 minutes; and so on. This is your Lost Time.

TIP

Harness and use your Lost Time. Prepare a list of small tasks that you can immediately turn to when you find yourself with some Lost Time and keep this list with you on the go, preferably in your smartphone.

Use the following as a guide to help you find and use your Lost Time:

Lost Time Examples	What you can use this time for
Your meeting finishes 10 minutes early You have 10 minutes between patients Sitting waiting for the dentist	Network: on your smartphone, maintain a list of key contacts you would like to stay in touch with but who you don't often reach out to for lack of time. When you make a call, frame the conversation to manage both your and your contact's time; for example: *Hi Rob, I was just thinking about you and found I had 10 minutes to spare between consults. How are you?* Your Lost Time is a terrific way to stay in touch with your network. Dictate into your smartphone bullet points from the meeting you just attended. Take a toilet break or make a cup of tea. Read a journal article. Dictate text messages to staff delegating actions from the meeting. Call your partner to say *Hi* Grab a piece of fruit. Get up and stretch your legs.

Commuting to and from work by public transport	Listen to an audio book.
	Listen to Continuing Professional Development podcasts.
	Undertake online research.
	Book your next holiday.
	Order flowers for someone special.
	Brainstorm gifts for an upcoming birthday or anniversary. Buy the card and wrapping paper at the next newsagent you pass and where possible order the gift online.
	Book your next car service.
Commuting to and from work by car	Batch personal/catch-up phone calls.
	Batch phone call meetings with colleagues.
	Batch time to return phone calls.
	Batch staff catch-ups and manage via phone; e.g. if you travel 20 minutes to and from work each day, schedule one x 1:1 in the morning and one x 1:1 in the afternoon.
	Make a reservation for date night.
	Call your mum!
	Dictate reports, letters and emails.
	(In all cases, only make hands-free calls)
Stuck in traffic	Dictate reports, letters and emails.
	(Use a headset connected to your phone to ensure hands-free)
Walking between your office and hospital rounds	Power walk, which doubles as exercise.
	Batch time to listen to phone messages.
Waiting for a patient to be prepped for surgery	Dictate a draft post-op report into your phone which can be corrected/completed after the surgery.

Commitment – only attend the right meetings

> Better to prevent than regret
> — Salvadorian Proverb

How many hours a week do you spend in meetings? Maybe a better question is, how many hours a week do you spend in *productive* meetings?

This one is a great quick win. If meetings seem to be taking over your working life, it's time to take Control.

Ask to see the Meeting Agenda prior to deciding whether to attend any meeting. It may be that the meeting is not relevant to you or is not worth your time spend. The only people who need to be at a meeting are the decision makers. If this is not you then politely decline.

> **TIP**
>
> Keep minuting simple and action-based: *What* (what is the action), *When* (when is the action due) and *Who* (who will take the action).

When you convene a meeting, remember that a quick meeting is a good meeting. Meetings do not need to go for an hour. It is better to hold short meetings to discuss one or two agenda items than one very long meeting rushing through ten agenda items.

> **TIP**
>
> Schedule standing-up meetings or walking meetings. The former will result in a quicker meeting while the latter allows you to get some exercise and fresh air at the same time.

Commitment – say No

If you are a *Yes* person and find it hard to say *No*, never forget that your time is money (you know your hourly rate from Step 3: Analyse).

> **TIP**
>
> If your time is worth $100 an hour and you spend 6 hours a week doing for others what they could do for themselves, that's $600 worth of your time (your Financial Cost).

When someone asks you to do something for them, they are essentially asking you for a favour, and it will cost you (at least at a Financial or Lost Opportunity level, and possibly at an Emotional and/or Physical level). If you want to perform the favour, that's great! It's a simple *Yes*. But, what if you don't?

Take Control and make the Commitment to just say *No*. For the more squeamish, remind yourself that every time you say *Yes* to someone (when you really would rather not) you are saying *No* to yourself and something you want to do.

> **TIP**
>
> If someone on the street stopped you and asked you for $50 what would you say? *No!* And yet, when someone you know stops and asks you for some (or a lot) of your time, you often say *Yes*. Think it through.

Try a response like this:

Polite? Tick. You haven't committed your precious time to something you don't want to do? Tick. You haven't over-committed? Tick. You have left the door open if *you* change your mind? Tick. You won't be chased because you have taken control of the follow up? Tick.

The reality for some, however, is that it can be hard to say *No* because it is human nature to not want to disappoint. If you are not comfortable with a straight out *No*, a useful strategy is to give an immediate positive response closely followed by a negative – that is – *Yes, However, No*. The initial *'Yes, that sounds great'* immediately gratifies the listener with a positive comment (which is what they were after), but ultimately the answer really is '*… but only on my terms.'*

The potential downside of this strategy is that the person asking for the favour may well be prepared to wait it out and have you commit your time on your terms. Damn them.

If this is the case, it's time to suck it up and revert to a straight out *No*.

Commitment – the pivot

One stone, two birds — Japanese proverb

Not every Deadline in your Calendar is set in concrete; this is the reality. You can't Control absolutely everything. From time to time influences outside your control will throw a spanner in the works and upset your next half hour, hour, day, etc. The key is to Control what you can - be agile and have the ability to pivot to accommodate and even benefit from the unplanned occurrence.

Example

Dr YoHan has a scheduled 30-minute online consult with a patient with a unique medical issue. In preparation, he has undertaken specialised research and prepared a comprehensive checklist of the medical information he wants to cover. At the eleventh hour the consult is cancelled by the patient. Rather than moving on to his next consult - or far worse, killing 30 minutes of his time - aka Lost Time - Dr YoHan pivots and spends the time turning his research notes into a Medical Blog. This will be of interest to his colleagues and will contribute to his credibility as an expert in this area, also possibly allowing him to increase his hourly rate.

Commitment – eliminate interruptions

Two roads overcame the hyena
— Swahili Proverb

Interruptions at work come in the form of digital distraction (phone calls, emails), human distraction (questions, meetings, chit chat) and self-distraction (where you lack Commitment and actively seek out distractions rather than work).

Unfortunately, interruptions are unavoidable in the medical profession where patient care could otherwise be compromised. However, there is a fine line as interruptions can add significantly to cognitive load, increase stress, inhibit decision-making performance and increase task errors. Moreover, for doctors, interruptions are not just about frustration or lost productivity. For you, the constancy of interruptions you experience each day carry a significant overlay of risk that is not experienced in many other professions.

Obviously not all interruptions will be unwelcome, however every interruption you allow will cost you. Remember the Four Cost Layers?

On average, doctors are interrupted every 10 minutes and once interrupted it will take anything from a few minutes to 20 minutes to fully refocus on the original task. Assuming (generously) that each interruption takes just 2.5 minutes to resolve and then refocus from, at this rate you are losing just over 2 hours of productivity each day.

But it gets worse. Tasks which are interrupted are more likely to be completed quickly by taking shortcuts to make up for lost time. This is not a good outcome for any professional, let alone medical practitioners. So, while you need to be available to ensure safe patient care, it's important to establish the right balance between availability and, well, constant availability.

As doctors, some interruptions will be of the urgent, drop-everything kind. This is the nature of the profession. However, not all interruptions will require your urgent and immediate attention. Be honest. You will have a high degree of Control over non-urgent interruptions. And yet, each time you allow a non-urgent interruption to take you away from the task at hand, you are falling back into the bad time management habit of being reactive and, again, you lose Control of your time.

To Control interruptions, it helps to start by thinking in extremes – an interruption is anything in your day which you have not scheduled into your Calendar. Under this definition, an interruption will include unscheduled incoming phone calls, a colleague popping in and asking for 10 minutes of your time, unscheduled meeting requests, questions from your team, and so on. Start from this premise and then work towards a comfortable balance that puts you in Control of your time.

> **TIP**
>
> You won't be able to refuse all interruptions, but imagine how much time you could regain if you knocked back one in every three interruptions each day.

In finding your right tolerance or balance for managing interruptions, consider systemising interruptions on a triage basis to determine what types of interruption, and from whom, require your immediate attention. You can then establish a Practice-based Interruption Triage framework which you can share with your team to ensure all 'like' interruptions are managed consistently.

An example is set out below, the final column provides additional strategies you can implement to further assist your management of interruptions.

Example

Triage Table

Level	Triage	Coming from	Action	Examples
1	Emergency	My Team or Nursing Team	Interrupt immediately in person or via text, pager or call	Code Blue Family emergency

If emergency interruptions are commonplace, make your Calendar work for you; e.g. each day factor in a 30+ minute Batch to allow for the unexpected. While you can't identify the exact time an emergency will occur, a Batch of this nature gives you a buffer of time to play with when/if an emergency arises. In the event that an emergency doesn't occur you have regained 30+ minutes to allocate to the next task on your To Do List

Level	Triage	Coming from	Action	Examples
2	Enquiry	Practice Manager	Alert via text or email within 2–4 hours	A patient wants to discuss blood test results
				A colleague wants me to review a patient report

Develop standard messaging for your Practice Manager to text you. For example:

Template:

[x] query from [y]. Please respond to [mobile number] within 2-4 hours or provide me with update and I will contact [y]

Level	Triage	Coming from	Action	Examples
3	Admin	Practice Manager	Remind via email within 1–2 days	Change of practice hours for holiday period
				Sales Rep delivering 2 photocopiers for demonstration and then selection

When emailing you, your Practice Manager should use a clear Subject Line: Admin Reminder

Deal with these emails in a Process (low energy period) Email Batch.

If you work in an office environment, consider introducing an Office10-Minute Protocol, so that every hour on the hour everyone is available for a scheduled 10-minute period of interruption. Get up, walk around, ask what you need to ask and help your colleagues/team with what they need.

If you have a door, shut it and let your team know not to interrupt you when the door is shut (except for Emergencies).

Outside having systems such as the Interruption Triage Framework, if you decide to allow a particular interruption, first take a quick note of the stage you are at with the task at hand so that you can return to it more effectively and efficiently after the interruption.

Commitment – single-tasking

> He who begins too much, accomplishes little
> — German Proverb

Have you ever heard someone boast about how great they are at multitasking? Quite possibly this is a skill you pride yourself on having? If so, it's time to rethink this one.

Single-tasking is the art of completely focussing on one task (or one part of a large task) at a time, without interruption and until completion. It is the exact opposite of multitasking – the practice of juggling multiple tasks at the same time with the intention of trying to get more done in the time you have (for example, responding to an email while texting or allowing interruptions while working on a research paper, or taking a phone call while with a patient).

Unfortunately the ability to successfully multitask, while a wonderful skill, is possessed by only 2.5% of the human race. These beings are so rare that they are called *Supertaskers*. For the rest of us mere mortals, multitasking is fundamentally a stop-start-stop-start-stop-start random process of inefficiency. Can you pack a suitcase with your left hand and book accommodation on your smartphone with your right hand and mentally make a list of everything you need to do before your flight and pay attention to your 5 year old who is upset because she didn't get invited to a party? Of course you can. However the potential for error is high and costly.

> **TIP**
>
> Multitasking will cost you as much as 40% of your productivity as your brain attempts to quickly flip between competing tasks.

Moreover, multitasking is not a skill you can acquire through practice. Seriously, knock yourself out. It won't make one iota of difference. Accept this and move on.

Your best and only time management tool in this regard is a Commitment to single-tasking.

In your Calendar, Batch 45–60 minutes of your high energy time to spend on your Hairiest Task as identified from your To Do List. Prior to this block of time, do not check your device or open your emails. If you have a door, shut it. If you work in an open plan area, put on some sound reducing headphones or take your work somewhere quiet where you won't be interrupted or distracted. Turn your phone (unless on-call) and other alerts off and set a timer for 45–60 minutes to ensure your Commitment to focussed single-tasking.

As much as possible, pre-Batch your Calendar with similar periods of single-focussed work, spaced out across the day, followed by a short break.

Your day is not a marathon; it is a series of sprints. To work at your maximum efficiency, schedule regular breaks between each sprint. Efficient, focussed and productive periods of work punctuated by short periods of respite will be more valuable to you than longer periods of less productive work. Even a break of 5–10 minutes from a task will increase your Commitment and ability to single focus. Get up, stretch your legs, make a coffee, go to the toilet or grab some fresh air.

Commitment – SMART Delegation

> One bee cannot produce honey;
> one grain of rice cannot produce a meal
> — Japanese Proverb

From Step 3: Analyse you know that Delegation includes Insourcing and Outsourcing and from Step 4: Reframe you have decided exactly what you will Delegate at work and at home.

Delegation is not just a matter of allocating a task and hoping for the best. The key to getting the result you want by Delegating a task – you want the same or a better result than if you undertook the task yourself – is to give clear and proper instructions up front.

SMART Delegation will set your team members up for success, increasing the prospect that they will produce the right result the first time and minimising the amount of time you spend on supervision and/or rework.

SMART Delegation has 5 clear steps:

SMART Delegation Table

	Action	Note
SELECT	Select the best person to undertake the task.	
MOTIVATE	Explain why the task is important.	*This step is often missed when delegating. However it is critical to the success of the task that you explain to your team member why the work needs to be done, otherwise they are working on the task without context.*
ACTIVITY	Explain the details of the task.	
RESULT	Explain what a good result will look like.	*This is another critical step often missed when delegating. By explaining what a great result will look like, you are framing the task for your staff member and setting them up for success.*
TIME-FRAME	Set realistic, yet hard Deadlines for a mid-point check in, and then for final delivery. Schedule these Deadlines in your Calendar and put the task out of your mind.	

Example

Dr Sam has been asked to present a Keynote on advanced techniques in spinal surgery at an international medical conference. While she intends to deliver the Keynote, she decides to Delegate the research and first draft of the paper to a more junior doctor.

Using the SMART Delegation Framework:

Select: Dr Sam identifies Sarah, a new intern with a lot of promise.

Motivate: She explains to Sarah that there is an important opportunity to present to and engage a wider audience in discussion around cutting edge advancements in spinal surgery. She informs Sarah that she will be acknowledged as a co-author of the paper.

Activity: Dr Sam explains to Sarah that she needs her to undertake research into developments in spinal surgery over the last 24 months, with a focus on spinal tumours. Dr Sam wants Sarah to prepare the first draft of the presentation with an accompanying slide deck. Sarah needs to anticipate questions for the Q&A session and prepare draft responses, bios and an abstract for handing out at the conference.

Result: Dr Sam explains that a good result will include data from the USA, Australia, Singapore and Japan. It will cover the most recent thinking on different treatments and modalities such as chemotherapy, radiography and early surgery. The leading experts should be referenced. The Keynote should be timed to last 45 minutes, which is approximately 15 slides at Dr Sam's speaking pace, and allow time for questions. All data points should be clearly referenced in the slide deck.

Timeframe: Dr Sam wants the draft of the paper and slide deck in ten days time. She sends Sarah a Calendar invite for a 30 minute update in 5 days time and then again for an hour in 10 days time to take her through the draft materials. Then Dr Sam puts the activity out of her mind.

Example

Dr Diana's medical practice is celebrating its 5-year Anniversary and she wants to celebrate. She loves a good party, but planning this will take hours. She decides to Delegate the task and then stay out of the way.

Using the SMART Delegation Framework:

Select: *She asks for a volunteer from the team, a great way for the best party-planner to self-select. John puts his hand up for the job.*

Motivate: *She explains to John that she wants a party specifically celebrating the success of the Practice, to reward the team, and to thank their partners for their support.*

Activity: *She wants John to organise a dinner party for 20 guests including partners, within a budget of $8000, including a gift for staff. Plus something fun, like a karaoke machine. John needs to keep all the details secret.*

Result: *A great result will be a lovely dinner, followed by dancing and singing, where everyone feels special.*

Timeframe: *Dr Diana locks in 30 July for the event, and asks John to take her through the final details 2 weeks before. Then she puts the task out of her mind.*

Checklist: Now You Know

The following productivity strategies will help you maintain your Commitment to performing the right tasks at the right time with absolute focus:

- ☐ Planning for your Lost Time to ensure you use all of your time well
- ☐ Managing meetings
- ☐ How to say *No*, or at least how not to say *Yes*
- ☐ Eliminating interruptions
- ☐ Increasing your productivity with single-tasking
- ☐ SMART Delegation

Your First Aid Kit

Tell me, I will forget. Show me, I will remember. Involve me, I will understand — Chinese Proverb

SMART Time Management for Doctors is intended to inform and educate you on how to better manage your time, to move you from functioning in a reactive mode to functioning in a proactive mode. You now have everything you need to regain significant control of your time.

Having said that, some readers will prefer to engage a coach to guide and push them. A great time management Coach is like a great Personal Trainer - *you know you can jog around the block yourself, but your PT will make you run faster than you thought you could and will then add 20 burpees, 30 push-ups and 50 sit-ups to really get you the results you want.* Similarly, a great time management Coach will push you to ensure your success.

If you want to know more about how Kate Christie can work with you individually or with your Practice or hospital to maximise your productivity, send an email to info@timestylers.com with your contact details and she will discuss coaching, workshop and education options with you.

About Kate Christie

Kate Christie, Founder and CEO of Time Stylers, is a Time Management expert, International Speaker and bestselling Author.

Kate has appeared on television and radio, and in print, as a leading commentator on managing work/life integration and time management and productivity techniques to ensure people can have success across their career, family, community and life.

Kate is a mum to three amazing teenagers. Prior to having children, she was a lawyer and senior executive who worked hard and had the energy, confidence and focus to back herself and grow her career. She simply flew up that corporate ladder with her fist clenched to smash through the glass ceiling! Things became more challenging after Kate had 3 babies under 3.5 years of age. Time Management became a big focus.

Kate's authenticity is one of her greatest assets, but be aware that she doesn't do warm and fuzzy. Her focus is on ensuring her audience is left educated and entertained, and most importantly, with a lasting impact on the way they choose to live, work and do business.

SMART Time Management for Doctors is Kate's second book. Her first book *Me Time: The Professional Woman's Guide to Finding 30 Guilt-free Hours a Month* is an Amazon bestseller.

About Time Stylers

The Time Stylers approach is practical: to combine coaching, education and strategies to create, build and sustain a much smarter personal time management framework to free up hours of your precious time to live the life you want.

Individual Doctors:

Working through the content of this book can be challenging. If you know you will achieve better and faster results by having a coach work with you, please visit www.timestylers.com to review the range of programs to support you:

Do It Yourself: For content which includes recorded guidance from Kate opt for the online course matching each step of *The 5 SMART Steps*. Kate's upbeat style works well to supplement the book's content. For more information go to www.timestylers.com

Done With You: Kate periodically holds Workshop Intensives. Individuals are welcome, as well as professional couples and groups from any discipline. There is pre-work to complete, and these Workshops include rigorous work and decision making. Enquire at info@timestylers.com.

Done For You: To apply to work discreetly and directly with Kate as your personal Time Styler, enquire by email at info@timestylers.com.

Medical Teams:

Kate is available to conduct SMART Time Management Workshops for your team. If you would like to book Kate to work with your team, contact her at info@timestylers.com.

Medical and Pharmaceutical Conferences:

Kate can be engaged to speak at your next National or International Conference. If you would like to book Kate as a Keynote Speaker at your next Medical Conference or event, contact her at keynote@timestylers.com.

Testimonials

Juggling the demands of being a doctor and mother of four, I thought that constant exhaustion and guilt were inevitable. Kate' Christie's 5 SMART Steps guided me through the process of achieving real and sustainable change. I improved my productivity while reclaiming much needed family and personal time. There are a myriad of general time management books but Smart Time Management for Doctors identifies and helps with issues specific to medical practitioners. Kate's description of my work and family life was uncannily accurate - I kept wondering if she had a webcam set up! I cannot recommend this book highly enough!

> — *Geeta, Gastroenterologist and Hepatologist,*
> *B Sci.(Hnns) M.B.B.S(Hons) M.R.C.P.(UK) F.R.A.C.P.*

Kate Christie makes time management simple and logical. Her framework - The 5 SMART Steps is easy to understand and apply and can readily be transferred to a shift working timetable. The framework is invaluable when it comes to optimising examination preparation, particularly when juggling study with full time work. As incredibly busy doctors often working in highly stressful environments, having smart strategies to find 'Me Time' or simply just 'time out' is key for maintaining a healthy and mindful work/ life balance. I recommend SMART Time Management for Doctors to busy medical practitioners everywhere.

> — *Katherine, Provisional Anaesthetic Fellow, BSc (Hons) PhD MBBS*

Kate draws fully on her previous experience as a busy professional alongside busy family roles to outline an approach to time management that is accessible, clear and practical. In SMART Time Management for Doctors she directs her timely wisdom to an especially busy group of health professionals who are sometimes tending to others health and wellbeing at the expense of their own. This book is a boon for busy health professionals seeking a better balance.

> — *Chris, Clinical Psychologist, Fellow of The Australian Psychological Society*

Kate Christie has written a book which shines the light on the unique time management challenges faced by doctors. Her 5 SMART Steps is a logical and simple to follow framework which all doctors can use to regain significant control over their time. I commend the skill, tenacity and veracity of this book which is pithy, punchy and can fulfil its intention of helping us doctors reclaim some of that precious time!

— Mukesh Haikerwal, General Practitioner,
Former President of the Australian Medical Association,
Chair of the AIHW, M.B.; Ch.B

Kate Christie makes time management simple and logical. With the 5 Smart Steps I am changing the way I manage my time and facing the challenge of 'filing and not piling'. The enjoyment and value of raising self sufficient, independent adults cannot be underestimated.

— Diana, Paediatrician MBBS FRACP

Kate Christie is truly one of a kind - I've never met anyone so incredibly passionate and so hugely capable when it comes to helping people take control of their time - the number one issue we all face in life.

Kate is a bestselling author, international speaker, she's appeared on Australian and NZ television, she has been featured on radio and in print as a leading commentator on time management and managing work/life integration. '

Her laser like focus is to help people take control of their time to ensure more meaningful success across career, family, community, and life. Having consulted to big and small business, government departments, and high level executives, Kate has now delivered the definitive workbook to help Doctors gain control of their time.

My advice is simple, if you're a Doctor or work in the medical industry take the time to read everything Kate does. Her advice really does have the potential to change your life. Many people promise this, few deliver, Kate Christie most certainly does!

— Andrew Griffiths, International Bestselling Author and Global Speaker.

www.ingramcontent.com/pod-product-compliance
Lightning Source LLC
Chambersburg PA
CBHW070731220326
41598CB00024BA/3383